...tioned in
...tight, w/
...front. Black

...ANTASTIC!

→

...I'm going
...ng machine
...home. sort
...tandish
...them.
TO DO ME
: y'know
...ready.
Well, I'll
...more
...to have
...around.

SIGH!!! AND A F...
GAVE ME A DRES...
WEAR FOR THE OCCASION — A
WINE-COLORED VELVET, OLD, FROM
A GOODWILL STORE, BUT BEAUTIFUL!

QUEEN ANNE KIND OF
SLEEVES & A VERY
LOW & BROAD NECKLINE.
REALLY PANTASTIC.

NOW, I HAVE A PROBLEM.
I'M HOPING THE CHICAGO JOB
WILL RESOLVE IT FOR ME, BUT
RIGHT NOW IT'S PLAGUING ME.
LAST WEEKEND WE PLAYED IN
THE CITY & A MAN FROM
ELECTRA, A <u>GOOD</u> LABEL, SPOKE
TO ME AFTERWARDS. LIKED ME/US
A LOT. DURING THE WEEK, SOMEONE
CALLED ME.... SEEMS ROTHCHILD
(THE GUY FROM ELECTRA, WHO
DISCOVERED PAUL BUTTERFIELD
WHO IS <u>VERY</u> BIG NOW — HE

Janis Joplin

Janis Joplin

A Performance Diary
1966 - 1970

Acid Test Productions

Acid Test Productions
1370 Industrial Avenue, Suite G
Petaluma, CA 94952
(707) 769-7484
800.600.5744
AcidTest@ix.netcom.com

Printed in Hong Kong

10 9 8 7 6 5 4 3 2 1

ACKNOWLEDGMENTS

The publishers would like to thank the following for their contributions: Laura Joplin, Del Furano, Dean Gelfand, Joseph Bongiovi, Jacaeber Kastor, Phillip Cushway, Jerry Pompili, Sylvia Bellucci, John Cooke, David Dalton, Bob Weir, David Getz and Gail Parenteau.

Table of Contents

Janis in Oz

by David Dalton

Among the virtual reality holograms in the Museum of Extreme Hipness, my particular favorite is Janis Joplin and Big Brother and the Holding Company from the summer of 1967. Big Brother was part of San Francisco's trinity of celestial bands — along with the Grateful Dead and Quicksilver Messenger Service — and Janis was their lead singer from 1966 to 1968.

I enter a small booth in the section called Artifacts of the First Great Psychedelic Era. From the POP SAINTS file I select BIG BROTHER AND THE HOLDING COMPANY. The voice prompt tonelessly advises me to "select from concert menu for access to rock-band tableaux." I scroll through a long list of Big Brother performances, skipping over ZENEFIT AT AVALON BALLROOM WITH GRATEFUL DEAD AND QUICKSILVER MESSENGER SERVICE NOVEMBER 13, 1967 and MONTEREY POP JUNE 17 & 18, 1967. I find what I'm looking for and enunciate my

choice carefully into the synchromike: "Summer Solstice Celebration, Golden Gate Park, June twenty-first, nineteen sixty-seven."

And there, hovering, suspended in the center of the hologram, is Janis, beautiful and radiant as I remember her most vividly from the summer of 1967: top hat and hippie threads, striped engineer's pants tied with a multicolored Peruvian sash, beads and baubles cascading over her T-shirt, rings encrusting her fingers, countless bracelets encircling her arms. The image is dominated by that face, the face of an ageless childlike goddess that fills the blue void of the hologram like a Japanese moon.

On the soundtrack is a tape of an interview with Janis that I had conducted in a dingy bar near the Louisville airport. Janis is saying,

The Summer Solstice. . . . Yeah, we walked over to Haight Street and bought some wine, me and Sunshine [Pat Nichols] and our dog George. We walked, sauntered, *sashayed* to Haight Street and bought a jug, that's all I remember. I think I met [Hell's Angel] Freewheelin' Frank that day, too. Some of the Angels are real good friends of mine—Sweet William, Crazy Pete. Freewheelin' I met a long time ago, Moose is a good friend. I don't really know too many others, as evidenced by the fact that I got punched out by a bunch of them at a dance I played for them.

A background slowly fills in behind her: an old tree, hippies dancing in a circle, a parachutist slowly falling to earth. Janis is now standing in front of an elongated forties limousine, smoking a cigar and taking swigs from a bottle. Among all the images that remain from that day — a sea of painted faces, Harlequins from the San Francisco Mime Troupe, hordes of smoldering Angels, self-anointed shamans, wagon masters, demons, medieval damsels, bodhisattvas, naked children clutching balloons, space walkers, chromosome divers — Janis seems both the most fantastic and the most real. Perhaps it is that among all the impersonations in the park that afternoon, hers was the most plausible.

In the midst of all this insanity, a motorcycle cop, his boot on the running board, writes out a ticket in all seriousness for "an illegally parked vehicle in a public place." As Janis catches sight of him, she taps her cigar and gingerly moves around the curves of the old limousine with the deliberate trajectory of a planet, swaying in that articulated gait that always made W. C. Fields look as if he were trying to stand up in a small rowboat.

I see myself approaching her, asking if I can take a photograph of her with Big Brother. "To tell you the truth, honey, I don't know where the boys went to," she says in her croaky little-girl voice, her face serious as an old plate. The image wobbles and recedes rapidly, telescoping to a small, round disk of light as if it had been sucked back into the vacuum of time, leaving only Janis's ear-to-ear grin floating across the clear blue sky of the afternoon like the smoky trace of the Cheshire cat.

As this first picture evaporates, it is replaced almost immediately with images in saturated colors that dance before my eyes to the opening busy-sawmill drone of Big Brother's guitars and ecstatic yelping. I see Jimi Hendrix, an agile, numinous figure in an embroidered Moroccan vest, pink ruffled shirt, vaquero hat, and crushed velvet pants clambering onto the back of Big Brother's sound truck to shoot Polaroids with a camera he has fixed to take

Big Brother and the Holding Company playing at McNear's Beach, San Rafael, Ca., 1967.
© Baron Wolman.

only double exposures. Janis, sensual, ripe, and fiery, is dancing barefoot like a gypsy, delirious with pleasure as she moves rhythmically to the accompaniment of her own singing.

Midsong — mid–"No-no-no-no-no, beh-beeee" — she spies Jimi and with comic theatricality clasps her hands to her heart and looks heavenward. With a kind of anything-that-comes-along-belongs-in-this-song *Sprechgesang,* she incorporates him into the lyric: "B-b-b-but I just can't believe it, man" — — Dave Getz does a little drumroll punctuating her Mad Hatter monologue — "my idol, Jimi Hendrix, *sigh!*" With both hands, Jimi blows her a kiss, and Janis launches into the song again. But it's no longer that mean ol' mistreatin' mama blues. It's taken on a decidedly gospel-tinged evangelist-of-love fervor: "Just honey, honey, hon-eeeee, when I thought my man was gone, you comin' 'round and I know you gonna stay, stay, stay by me all night long, beh-beh, because if ya don't, honey, you know it just ain't ri-i-i-i-i-i-ight!"

Jimi is grinning his big-bad-wolf grin as Noel Redding, his bass player, drags him away. Although Noel, too, is tripping, he knows Jimi's propensity for distraction — for getting drawn into anything that crosses his path — and here they are on the sound stage of a mad opera where every conceivable line between reality and pure 200-miked insanity has been erased and there's Janis, the living, breathing R. Crumb special, and it's all *so perfect* and, given the synapse-snapping current that is saying *yes! yes! yes!* every twelve nanoseconds, anything, really, could happen. LIVE! ON STAGE! SEE JANIS JOPLIN & JIMI HENDRIX REALLY GET DOWN! It's tempting, but someone has to play nanny, and as Noel pulls Jimi away, Janis and Jimi mime the desperation of children suddenly wrenched away from a game of make-believe.

Shouting, screaming, dancing kids are swarming in the wake of Big Brother's sound truck. On the truck bed, Janis sings her raunchy blues like nursery rhymes. Little groups of awestruck youngsters stare vacantly at this mirage from the dusty area in front of the truck. A figure leans over the edge of the truck, grinning like a hookah, his features distorted by the focus of memory so that the tip of his nose is all that remains of reality. He is passing out handfuls of joints rolled from grass planted on that spot earlier in the year. The VR image of Big Brother begins to oscillate and decompose.

To me, that morning and afternoon will always seem magically suspended, as if somehow removed from the onward rush of events, and at the center of the time warp is Janis — radiant, earthy, and vulnerable. As the solstice revelers — weary of wonders like interplanetary visitors exhausted from their first day exploring earth — stumble, dance (to the bands still playing), and blow themselves into the sea at the edge of Golden Gate Park, and as the sun, wobbling on the edge of extinction, showers everything with flakes of rusty light, it seems for an instant that the original state of humankind must have resembled this day in its infinite possibilities, and that Janis, naive, filled with awe and ecstasy, could have been its first beautiful child.

—DAVID DALTON

Janis Joplin was real easy to take pictures
of, she exuded friendliness. Janis seemed
like she loved everybody; all you needed
was a camera and boom, magic!
— Clark Pierson

*Janis on Fifth Avenue, New York wearing a new
signature look, feather boas in her hair, May 1970.*
© Clark Pierson.

© Baron Wolman

"Didn't I make you feel like you were the only man,

Didn't I give you ev'rything that woman possibly can.
But with all the love I give you, it's never enough.
But I'm gonna show you, baby, that a woman can be tough.
So go on, go on, go on, go on, take it!
Take another little piece of my heart, now, baby. Break it!
Break another little piece of my heart now, honey."

You say that it's over, baby
You say that it's over now

And still you hang around now come on
Won't you move over

You know that I need a man
You know that I need a man
But when I ask you to just tell me
That maybe you can

Please don't do it to me babe
Please don't do it to me
Take the love I offer
Or let me be

I ain't quite ready for walking
I ain't quite ready for walking
And what will you do
with your life
Life just a dangling

Make up you mind
You're playing the fool
Make up your mind
You're playing the fool
Now either be my loving man
Or let me be

You can't disagree
You're playing with my heart
I believe you're toying with my affections
I can't take it no more
And furthermore I don't intend to
I'm tired of hanging from the end of a string
You expect me to fight like a God-damned mule

© Jay Good

© Herb Greene

© Herb Greene

Down on Me, Down on Me

Looks like everybody in this whole round
world
is down on me

Love in this world is so hard to find
When you've got yours and I've got mine
That's why it looks like everybody
in this whole round world
Is down on me

When you see a hand that's held out t'ward
you
Give it some love, some day it may be you
That's why it looks like everybody
in this whole round world
Is down on me

Believe in your brother, have faith in man
Help each other, honey, if you can
Because it looks like everybody
in this whole round world
Is down on me
Lord, down on me

© Jay Good

Big Brother, with the Orkustra
and the Grateful Dead,
New Year's Wail/Whale,
San Francisco, 1967

1

Janis and the Kozmic Blues
Band rehearse new material,
Jan. 2–Feb. 6, 1969

2

3

4

5

Big Brother, Sacramento
State College,
Sacramento, 1968

6

7

January

8

9

10

11

12

13

Big Brother, with Moby Grape
and The Morning Glory, Santa
Venetia Armory, San Rafael,
California, 1967

14

Big Brother, Human Be-In,
Golden Gate Park,
San Francisco, 1967

❝I came back to San Francisco and rock and roll had happened. Well, I'd never sung rock and roll, I sang blues — Bessie Smith kind of blues. They said, 'Janis, we want you to sing with these boys,' and I met them all, and you know how it is when you meet someone, you don't even remember what they look like you're so spaced by what's happening. I was in space city, man, I was scared to death. I didn't know how to sing the stuff, I'd never sung with electric music, I'd never sung with drums, I only sang with one guitar. I'd learned 'Down on Me.' It's a gospel song, and I'd heard it before and thought I could sing it, and they did the chords. So we practiced

© Jay Good

it all week, and they were working at the Avalon that weekend. They played a few numbers, and then they said, 'Now we'd like to introduce . . .'

"And nobody had ever heard of fuckin' me, I was just some chick, didn't have any hip clothes or nothing like that. I had on what I was wearing to college. I got on stage, and I started singing, whew! what a rush, man! A real, live, drug rush. I don't remember it at all, all I remember is the sensation — what a fuckin' gas, man. The music was boom, boom, boom! and the people were all dancing, and the lights, and I was standing up there singing into this microphone and getting it on, and whew! I dug it. So I said, 'I think I'll stay, boys.' Far out, isn't it? It sure did take me by surprise, I'll tell you. I wasn't planning any of this, I wasn't planning on sittin' in cold dressing rooms all my life, I didn't even know it existed.

"Even once I was a singer, I never wanted to be a star. I just liked to sing because it was fun, just like people like to play tennis, it makes your body feel good. Everybody gave you free beer. I don't remember much of the early period, we just worked around, all of us starving, I got some money from my parents. . . ."

—JANIS

Janis was born on January 19, 1943; under the sign of Capricorn. She was only mildly attached to the paraphernalia of astrology and psychedelia, although she did recognize in herself the affliction of that sign— intense introspection and the tendency to go from the heights of ecstacy to the depths of depression.

The goat on the peak, the fish in the deep.

January

15

Big Brother, with
the Merry Pranksters,
Shrine Auditorium,
Los Angeles, 1967

16

17

Big Brother, The Matrix,
San Francisco,
Jan. 17–22, 1967

18

☆ **19**

*Janis is born in
Port Arthur, Texas, 1943*

20

21

22

23

24

Big Brother, with the
Electric Flag and the
Youngbloods, Fillmore/
Winterland, San Francisco,
Jan. 25–27, 1968

25

26

Big Brother and the Holding Company; Big Mama Thornton; California Hall,
San Francisco, 1967. Artist: Michael Wood / Phxis Studios

27

28

January

29

30

31

"By 1966, the Haight with its outlaw fetishism was more than ready for Janis. She was almost a reincarnation of those salty gunslinging women of the Wild West. A blues-singing Calamity Jane! Janis didn't need to make up stories, she embodied them. You took one look at her and you made it up for her. In a matriarchal society like that of the Haight, Janis was the long-awaited diva."

—David Dalton

"Purity of action guided Janis's behavior. If she was going to be good,
she was very, very good. If she was going to be bad, she let all the stops out.
Anything less than full commitment to an idea or activity was 'hypocritical',
the worst adjective anyone could hurl at another."

— Laura Joplin, from *Love, Janis*

Janis with Andy Warhol and Tim Buckley at
Max's Kansas City restaurant, New York.
© Elliott Landy, LandyVision, Inc.

1

2

Big Brother and the Holding
Company, Cheetah,
Los Angeles, 1968

3

Big Brother, with Blue Cheer,
Hell's Angels dance, California
Hall, San Francisco, 1967

4

5

6

7

February

© Gene Anthony

"**I** was on stage and I looked out, and I knew they weren't ready. We were doing 'Piece of My Heart.' You know you can do a lot of different things; you know sometimes they get up spontaneously. Out in the Midwest they don't. They aren't supposed to stand up and they know it. It's hard to get 'em up. But I remember I was singing 'Piece of My Heart,' you know that 'Come on, well, come on' line — well, you know the guitar solo that leads into that part? I came in early, and I walked all the way to the front of the stage and shouted [in a hoarse whisper], 'Come on, come on!' and just fucking stamping my foot, and saying, 'I'm not going to sing anymore unless you do something,' you know, and they're going, 'Whoo-ooo-ooo, yes ma'am! Yes ma'am, yes ma'am!' A riot. Groovy.

"All they want is a little kick in the ass. You know, sometimes I jump off the stage and grab somebody and say, 'Let's dance.' When they reach a certain level, you know, they want to be lifted, but they're scared. Then all you gotta do is give the old kick in the ass, a big fucking kick in the ass, man. Then the promoters get goony, turn the lights on, pull the power, but by then it's all over [cackles]. I dig it! I dig it so much, man!"

— JANIS

Janis at Woodstock.
© Elliott Landy, LandyVision, Inc.

"It's a very sad thing. I love those guys more than anybody else in the whole world, they know that. But if I had any serious ideas of myself as a musician, I had to leave. Getting off, real feeling, that's the whole thing of music for me. But by the end, we were shucking. We worked four, six nights a week for two years, doing the same tunes, and we'd put everything into them we could. We just used each other up."

— JANIS, TALKING ABOUT BIG BROTHER AND THE HOLDING COMPANY

Kozmic Blues, University of
Vermont, Burlington, 1969

15

Big Brother, Palestra,
Philadelphia, 1968

16

Kozmic Blues, Toronto, 1969

Big Brother, with Quicksilver
Messenger Service, Avalon
Ballroom, San Francisco,
Feb. 17 & 18, 1967

17

Big Brother, Anderson Theatre,
New York City, 1968 — Big
Brother's first New York show

18

Big Brother, with Jefferson
Airplane, Fillmore Auditorium,
San Francisco, 1967

19

20

February

Kozmic Blues, Colby College,
Waterville, Maine, 1969

21

Janis is a "kind of mixture of Leadbelly, a steam engine, Calamity Jane, Bessie Smith, an oil derrick, and rotgut bourbon, funneled into the twentieth century somewhere between El Paso and San Francisco."
— Cashbox

Janis at the Detroit Airport, 1968
© Elliott Landy, LandyVision, Inc.

"When I'm there, I'm not here," Janis said later. *"I can't*

Big Brother, with MC5 and
Tiffany Shade, Grande
Ballroom, Detroit,
Mar. 1 & 2, 1968

1

*Big Brother and the Holding Company's first
album release on Mainstream,* Big Brother and
the Holding Company *1967*

Kozmic Blues Band, Duke
University, Durham, North
Carolina, 1969

2

Big Brother, with Steve Miller,
University of California
Medical Center,
San Francisco, 1967

3

4

5

6

Kozmic Blues, Evanston,
Illinois, 1969

7

March

Big Brother and the Holding Company;
MC5 Grande Ballroom, Detroit, 1968.
Artist: Gary Grimshaw.

8   Big Brother, with Tim Buckley
     and Albert King, Fillmore East,
     New York City, 1968

9   Big Brother, Wesleyan
     University, Middletown,
     Connecticut, 1968

     Kozmic Blues, Toledo,
     Ohio, 1969

10

11

12   Big Brother, with Country Joe
     and the Fish, Steve Miller
     Blues Band, and Quicksilver
     Messenger Service, Sunflower-
     Phoenix Dance Benefit for Aid
     to Vietnam and Mississippi,
     Fillmore Auditorium,
     San Francisco, 1967

13

14

The Blues
According to Janis

by John Byrne Cooke

"Been down so long, it looks like up to me . . ."

The blues is a moan of pain and a shout of joy. It's a sharecropper playing a shoebox guitar on the front porch in his work clothes, singing the blues because those are his Sunday-go-to-meetin' clothes, too, and it's B. B. King playing the same lick you've heard a hundred times but you still feel the blues in the same three notes. You sing the blues to keep from crying—or dying—and to celebrate your survival in the face of life's bad news. It's not an intellectual tradition. You either feel the blues or you don't.

Huddie Ledbetter—Leadbelly—was the first to get to Janis through the blues. A Texas convict sent to a chain gang for manslaughter, he touched the soul of a Texas girl growing up on the comfortable, middle-class side of Port Arthur. She put a record on the turntable, and there he was, grabbing hold

Janis at the Anderson Theater, 1968.
© Elliott Landy, LandyVision, Inc.

of her with the blues. She had bad skin and felt like she didn't fit in. The blues gave her a home. Bessie Smith touched her, too, and Ma Rainey: women who had learned to sing in the dives and juke joints along alleys where the whores worked out of six-bit cribs. They set loose the music in Janis's heart and pushed her toward the bright lights.

Growing up, Janis lived in a clean house and wore clean clothes. Her father was an engineer for an oil company. Her mother was a teacher. They were educated, decent people. They passed on to Janis a fierce intelligence and encouraged her to nourish it, but no amount of education could cure her of the blues.

She sang the joy as well as the sadness. She sang it loud and long. Her joy reached out and touched a generation that was hungry for something besides the platitudes of the 1950s. A generation whose parents lied to them about drugs and sex and success and security and the American way, and who wanted to hear the truth. Janis sang the truth and they made her a star.

Handbill for Big Brother and the Holding Company, Tim Buckley. Fillmore East, N.Y. 1968 © Bill Graham Presents Artist: Charles Brandwynn / Photographer: Linda Eastman

Big Brother and the Holding Company, Love Rock Garden,
San Francisco, 1966
Artist: Michael Wood / Pyxis Studios

March

15

Big Brother, Electric Factory,
Philadelphia,
Mar. 15–17, 1968

Kozmic Blues, blocking for
"The Ed Sullivan Show" in
the morning; appearance at
University of Michigan, Ann
Arbor in the evening, 1969

16

Kozmic Blues, appearance on
"The Ed Sullivan Show,"
1969

17

Big Brother, with Charles
Lloyd and the Sir Douglas
Quintet, Avalon Ballroom,
San Francisco,
Mar. 17 & 18, 1967

18

19

20

Kozmic Blues, Winterland/
Fillmore West,
Mar. 20–23, 1969

21

Big Brother, with Citizens for
Interplanetary Activities
(C.I.A.), The Rock Garden,
San Francisco,
Mar. 21–25, 1967

Big Brother, Cheetah,
Chicago, Mar. 22–24, 1968

22

23

24

25

26

Kozmic Blues,
Sacramento, 1969

27

March

Kozmic Blues,
San Bernardino, 1969

28

© Elliott Landy, LandyVision, Inc.

"I'm a victim of my own insides. There was a time when I wanted to know everything. I read a lot. I guess you'd say I was pretty intellectual. It's odd, I can't remember when it changed. It used to make me very unhappy, all that feeling. I just didn't know what to do with it. But now I've learned how to make feeling work for me. I'm full of emotion and I want a release, and if you're on stage and if it's really working and you've got the audience with you, it's a oneness you feel. I'm into me, plus they're into me, and everything comes together. You're full of it. I don't know, I just want to feel as much as I can, it's what 'soul' is all about."

— *JANIS*

March 1967

Dear Mother . . . .

. . . So far, moving into the city has really hung us up — we have no rehearsal hall. Very hard to find a place where you can make a lot of noise, don't have to pay much rent, and the equipment will be safe overnight. . . .Janis

Kozmic Blues, San Diego,
1969

29

Kozmic Blues, departure
for Stockholm and European
tour, 1969

30

Big Brother, with the
Charlatans and Blue Cheer,
Avalon Ballroom,
San Francisco,
Mar. 31 & Apr. 1, 1967

31

March

Oh, Lord, won't you buy me a Mercedes Benz?

My friends all drive Porsches,
I must make amends.
Worked hard all my lifetime, no help
from my friends,
So, Lord, won't you buy me a Mercedes
Benz?

Oh, Lord, won't you buy me a
color TV?
"Dialing for Dollars" is trying to
find me.
I wait for delivery each day until
three,
So, Lord, won't you buy me a
color TV?

Oh, Lord, won't you buy me a night on
the town?
I'm counting on you, Lord, please
don't let me down;
Prove that you love me and buy the
next round.
Oh, Lord, won't you buy me a night on
the town?

Ev'rybody: Oh, . . .

MERCEDES BENZ By Janis Joplin, Michael McClure and
Bobby Neuwirth, © 1970 Stong Arm Music

Janis in the performer's pavilion at Woodstock.

© Elliott Landy, LandyVision, Inc.

Kozmic Blues Band, taping
of television show in
Stockholm, 1969

1

Big Brother and the Holding
Company, Generation, New
York City, Apr. 2–7, 1968

2

Kozmic Blues, flight to
London for European tour
rehearsals, 1969

3

4

Janis sings with Big Brother
at a reunion performance,
San Francisco, 1970

5

6

7

Big Brother, with Jimi
Hendrix, Buddy Guy,
Joni Mitchell, Richie Havens,
Paul Butterfield, and Elvin
Bishop, Wake for Martin
Luther King, Jr., Generation,
New York City, 1968

© 1997 Daniel Kramer

Big Brother and the Holdiing Company; Jack the Ripper,
The Ark, Sausalito, 1967

Big Brother and the Holding Company

by John Byrne Cooke

Big Brother and the Holding Company was one of the seminal San Francisco rock bands. Together with the Jefferson Airplane, the Grateful Dead, and Quicksilver Messenger Service, they originated the San Francisco Sound. Keeping the back beat and raw voice of the blues, these bands took rock and roll into the stratosphere, reaching for the ethereal sounds of the outer limits.

At the outset, they were "family" bands, living together in communal houses, sharing decisions and income equally. Their philosophy was a conscious rejection of the star system and the business world of popular music. Their music was both pied piper and camp follower to a growing social experiment in alternative lifestyles that made San Francisco the city that most visibly symbolized the rebellion of the sixties.

Big Brother and the Holding Company © Herb Greene

© Herb Greene

The music, the anything-goes experimentation, and the rebellion suited Janis to a T. San Francisco and Big Brother welcomed the wandering Texas girl and gave her a home. From the first moment she took center stage with the band, she captivated audiences by her ability to express pain and uncertainty, her determination to have a good time and try anything that might lead to a life more honest and real than the play-it-safe middle-class existence our parents cherished.

When the band ventured beyond San Francisco the press lionized Janis and neglected the boys who had founded it. The *New York Times* proclaimed, "Janis Joplin is climbing fast in the heady rock firmament" and called her "as remarkable a new pop-music talent as has surfaced in years." Tensions first unspoken, then shouted, fractured the harmony within the group. From outside the band came suggestions that Janis should leave them behind and reach for superstardom on her own. Big Brother symbolized for her the community and life she had adopted and wanted desperately to remain a part of. She loved them, but in the end she decided to leave them. She chose a difficult path with potentially greater rewards—and much greater risks—and she suffered the painful consequences of her decision long before glimpsing the joy she was seeking.

15 Big Brother, with the New Breed, Civic Auditorium, Stockton, California, 1967

16

17 Kozmic Blues, Stockholm, 1969

18

19 Big Brother, with the Mint Tattoo, Selland Arena, Fresno, California, 1968

Kozmic Blues, Tivoli Gardens, Copenhagen, 1969

20 Big Brother, Santa Barbara, 1968

Big Brother, with Howlin' Wolf, Fillmore Auditorium, San Francisco, Apr. 21 & 22, 1967

21 Kozmic Blues, Albert Hall, London, 1969 (sold out)

Monterey

by John Byrne Cooke

Photos by © Gene Anthony

The American audience fell in love with Janis Joplin on a foggy June afternoon in 1967 at the County Fairgrounds in Monterey, California. In the course of a single song, she gained ten thousand fans. If she had plummeted from the low clouds in a space ship, her impact couldn't have been greater.

The Monterey International Pop Festival was the first of the late, great rock festivals. It was smaller than many that followed, but it had an essential joy and purity that was never equaled. Police and community fears about an invasion of hippies evaporated as the music began and a gossamer enchantment settled over the fairgrounds. The spell lasted until the festival was over and the crowd disbanded, each person carrying a piece of the music's intangible spirit out into the world.

The theme of the show was music, love, and flowers. The music was a sure thing. For three days, a succession of headliners would step onto the

Fairgrounds stage and give it their all. The flowers were flown in from Hawaii by the planeload. Pink orchids everywhere. The love was speculative. It was a hope. A prayer. You couldn't ship it in or conjure it up. Can't buy me love. But it was there from the start.

The festival's promoters were from Los Angeles. They were aware of the explosion of the outer-limits rock sounds coming from San Francisco, but the program leaned heavily on the reigning stars of popular music: the Mamas and the Papas, Simon and Garfunkel, The Who. Big Brother and the Holding Company, the least well known of the San Francisco bands, was scheduled only for a short appearance on the Saturday afternoon matinee.

They came on stage, four *long*-haired young men and Janis, equally long-haired and outfitted in a gold lamé pantsuit. The set culminated with Janis's show-stopper from the San Francisco ballrooms, Willie Mae "Big Mama" Thornton's "Ball and Chain." When Janis hit the first chorus, the audience felt its collective breath stop in its throat. Can a white girl sing the blues like this? Janis's answer was an emphatic *Yes!* In response to the enthusiastic ovation, and so D. A. Pennebaker's multi-camera film crew could recapture the astonishing performance from all angles, the schedule was shuffled so Big Brother could play again on Sunday evening. Again Janis triumphed. Even before that second appearance, everyone knew that Janis's performance was the one they would never forget.

The Monterey Pop Festival was a transcendent moment. Naive in our enthusiasm, we thought it was the dawning of the Age of Aquarius. As things turned out, it was its high point. For Janis, Monterey was a launching pad. It marked the sudden brilliant dawning of her career, from which there was no turning back.

© Gene Anthony

22

23

Big Brother, with the Charles
Lloyd Quartet, California Hall,
San Francisco, 1967

24

Kozmic Blues, return to the
United States from
European tour, 1969

25

Big Brother, The Matrix, San
Francisco, Apr. 25–27, 1967

Kozmic Blues, Springfield,
Massachusetts, 1969

26

Big Brother, Foothill College,
Los Altos Hills, California, 1968

Kozmic Blues, MIT, Cambridge,
in the afternoon; Brown
University, Providence, Rhode
Island, in the evening, 1969

27

Big Brother, San Bernardino,
1968

Kozmic Blues, Rochester,
New York, 1969

28

Big Brother, with Big Mama
Thornton, California Hall,
San Francisco,
Apr. 28 & 29, 1967

April

© 1997 Daniel Kramer

29

30

Big Brother begins recording
Cheap Thrills album in
Los Angeles,
Apr. 29–May 9, 1968

Dope, Sex, and Cheap Thrills

by John Byrne Cooke

"Dope, sex, and cheap thrills" was a theme R. Crumb expounded in his raunchy, funny, underground comix as joyously as "Keep on truckin' the blues away," which was usually accompanied by a three-panel sequence of Mr. Natural walking the walk, grinning the grin, and generally looking like he hadn't had the blues since sometime well before dawn last week.

Janis and the boys in Big Brother loved Crumb's cartoons, especially the Furry Freak Brothers. When they signed their record deal with Columbia records in November, 1967, they let it be known that they wanted to call the album *Dope, Sex, and Cheap Thrills*. Well, you can guess how Columbia felt about plastering an advertisement for dope and sex across the nation's music magazines, not to mention the album covers. In the end, they did go for *Cheap Thrills*, and they paid R. Crumb a pittance for his brilliant cover.

"In a sense, Cheap Thrills, the classic Janis Joplin and Big Brother and the Holding Company album, is itself a kind of primitive hologram of the high old days of Hippie City. For me, it distills better than anything else the exhilaration, funkiness, everything-leaping-out-at-you lunacy and kosmik koincidence of the Haight at its kaleidoscopic klimax. Everything about Cheap Thrills when it came out in August 1968 was celestial and goofy, starting with that great title and the rambunctious R. Crumb album cover in which everything has come to life in a tripping, rapping, bursting-out-of-its-seams exuberance. The album itself is a series of exquisitely ragged bluesy passion plays, complete with sound effects (complete with audience, actually). Even the 'vibes' from a seedy Los Angeles art bar (Barney's Beanery) get credited on the liner notes—and why not. And to top it off, the whole thing has the seal of approval of the 'Hell's Angels, Frisco.' A whole world crammed onto two sides of vinyl and a cardboard sleeve!"

— David Dalton

"I was the same chick, because I've been her forever, and I know her, and she ain't no star: she's lonely, or she's good at something. I have to get undressed after the show, my clothes are ruined, my heels are run through, my underwear is ripped, my body's stained from my clothes, my hair's stringy, I got a headache and I got to go home, and I'm lonely, and my clothes are all fucked up, my shoes have come apart, and I'm pleading with my road manager to please give me a ride home, please, please, just so I can take these fuckin' clothes off, and that ain't no star, man, that's just a person."
— *JANIS*

Big Brother, Chico State
College, Chico,
California, 1968

1

*Mid-May, Janis's first performance with her new band,
soon to be called the Full Tilt Boogie Band; Big Brother
and the Holding Company also plays, with Nick
Gravenites singing lead; Hell's Angels dance,
Pepperland, San Rafael, California, 1970*

Kozmic Blues Band, War
Memorial Auditorium,
Syracuse, New York, 1969

2

Big Brother, with Albert King,
Shrine Auditorium, Los
Angeles, May 3–4, 1968

3

Kozmic Blues,
Cornell University, Ithaca,
New York, 1969

Kozmic Blues, University of
New Hampshire,
Durham, 1969

4

Big Brother, with the Sir
Douglas Quintet and the
Orkustra, Avalon Ballroom,
San Francisco,
May 5–7, 1966

5

6

7

May

"If you can get them once, man, get them standing up when they should be sitting down, sweaty when they should be decorous, smile when they should be applauding politely . . . and I think you sort of switch on their brain, man, so that makes them say: 'Wait a minute, maybe I can do anything.' Whoooooo! It's life. That's what rock and roll is for, turn that switch on, and man, it can all be."

— JANIS

8

9

Kozmic Blues, Cleveland
Convention Center,
Ohio, 1969

10

Big Brother, Cal-Poly State
University, San Luis Obispo,
California, 1968

Kozmic Blues, Cobo Hall,
Detroit, 1969

11

Big Brother, with Country Joe
and the Fish, Fillmore
Auditorium,
San Francisco, 1967

Big Brother, with Bronze Hog,
Veterans Hall, Santa Rosa,
California, 1968

12

Kozmic Blues, Veteran's
Memorial Music Hall,
Columbus, Ohio, 1969

Big Brother, Winterland,
San Francisco,
May 12 & 13, 1967

13

Big Brother, with Taj Mahal
and Sweetwater,
San Fernando Valley State
College California, 1968

14

© Gene Anthony

May

15 Big Brother, with Rejoice and the Youngbloods, Hell's Angels dance, Carousel Ballroom, San Francisco, 1968

16

17 Big Brother, Freeborn Hall, University of California, Davis, 1968

18 Big Brother, San Jose Fairgrounds, San Jose, 1968

19 Big Brother, Pasadena, 1968

20 Big Brother records *Cheap Thrills* in Los Angeles, with some days off for R&R, May 20–June 12, 1968

21

Newsweek

MAY 26, 1969   50c

JANIS JOPLIN

Rebirth of the Blues

22

23

24

Big Brother, with the Clara
Ward Singers and H. P.
Lovecraft, Carousel Ballroom,
San Francisco,
May 24–26, 1968

25

26

Big Brother, with Steve Miller
Blues Band, Fillmore
Auditorium, San Francisco,
May 26 & 27, 1967

27

May

28

RENO, NEVADA
Colorful night view of fabulous casino row in
Virginia Street.

Spent the nite in Reno —
unfortunately the Nugget
was filled so I slept
in the back seat of my
car parked in a Reyal
gas station — but
still — a night in Reno!
Lost 60¢ in the slot
machines — phoo.
San Francisco by
noon. A letter
should arrive shortly XXX

Joplin
3130
Lombardy
Port Arthur,
Texas

THE
BATTLE-BORN
STATE
1864 ★ 1964

RENO, NEV
SEP 7

NEVADA
CENTENNIAL

NATURAL COLOR
by
Mike Roberts
BERKELEY 2, CALIF.

Distributed by Sierra News Company, Reno, Nevada

616036

SAN FRANCISCO
the City by the Golden Gate

5: SF-24

SAN FRANCISCO - OAKLAND BAY BRIDGE

The San Francisco-Oakland Bay Bridge is eight and one-quarter miles long. It was built at a total cost of $97,000,000. Its lofty span stretches from the anchorage in San Francisco to Yerba Buena Island, and continues to the eastern approaches of Oakland and Berkeley.

THURS - 10:30 A.M.

SIGH!!

XXX

address

Joplins
3130 Lombardy
Port Arthur
Texas

PUB. BY SMITH NEWS CO., 1338 MISSION ST., S. F. CALIF.

Postcards home from Janis, her first trip to California, 1964

May

29

Full Tilt, Gainesville, Florida, 1970

30

Big Brother, with the Jefferson Airplane, Quicksilver Messenger Service, the Charlatans, and the Grateful Dead, Benefit for the Haight-Ashbury Legal Organization, Winterland, San Francisco, 1967

Full Tilt, Jacksonville, Florida, 1970

31

Big Brother is filmed as part of the movie "Petulia," 1967

Full Tilt, Miami, 1970

"Chet Helms heard me one weekend up there. He was famous, he was one of the crazies that made it away from Texas at a very early age, he had split at eighteen. He was back in town, on the way to the West Coast from the East Coast—all Texans come back to Austin—and he heard me singing. He said, 'That girl's good, that girl's good.'

"I was wanting to leave, I was wanting to get the fuck out of there, but I didn't have quite enough nerve to leave by myself. Chet was leaving, and he said he wanted me to come with him, help him get rides. We hitchhiked to San Francisco, and we slept on a bunch of people's floors, and I sang a couple of times."

— JANIS

Janis with Chet Helms outside Pine Street apartment, San Francisco, 1967. © Herb Greene

Janis moves back to San Francisco from Austin, 1966

1

Big Brother and the Holding Company, with Country Joe and the Fish and Quicksilver Messenger Service, California Hall, San Francisco, Jun. 2 & 3, 1967

2

3

Janis joins Big Brother and the Holding Company, 1966

4

Full Tilt Boogie Band, Columbus, Ohio, 1970

5

6

Full Tilt, Indianapolis, 1970

7

June

DOWN ON ME
CALL ON ME - * closing
BLINDMAN - ...
ALL IS LONELINESS - faster
BYE BYE BABY *
EASY, ONCE YOU KNOW HOW
FAREWELL SONG - new feedback
BROWNSVILLE * new stop (5 ... before)
COMBINATION OF THE TWO - new entrance after break
LIGHT IS FASTER
I KNOW YOU RIDER
EASY RIDER
CUCKOO
BLOW MY MIND
MADMAN BLUES
SUMMERTIME ...
IT'S A DEAL - words for bridge ...
BALL & CHAIN
TURTLE BLUES *
ROADBLOCK
HALL OF MTN. KING
...THAT...
AMAZING GRACE
DRIVIN' STUPID
HALL
MAGIC OF LOVE - new break

663
8222

8   Big Brother, with Canned Heat, Avalon Ballroom, San Francisco, Jun. 8–11, 1967

9

10   First performance with Big Brother, Avalon Ballroom, San Francisco, 1966

11

12   Full Tilt, Louisville, Kentucky, 1970

13   Big Brother with the Foundations and Crazy World of Arthur Brown, Fillmore/ Winterland, San Francisco, Jun. 13–15, 1968

14   Full Tilt, Kansas City, 1970

Big Brother play list in handwriting of Janis, Dave Getz and other band members. Posted on the wall in the Lagunitis House.

June 6, 1966

Mother & Dad . . .

With a great deal of trepidation, I bring the news. I'm in San Francisco. Now let me explain — when I got to Austin, I talked to Travis Rivers who gave me a spiel about my singing w/a band out here. Seems Chet Helms, old friend, now is Mr. Big in S.F. Owns 3 big working Rock & roll bands with bizarre names like Captain Beefheart & his Magic Band, Big Brother & the Holding Co. etc. Well, Big Brother et al needs a vocalist. So I called Chet to talk to him about it. He encouraged me to come out — seems the whole city had gone rock & roll (and it has!) and assured me fame & fortune. I told him I was worried about being hung up out here w/no way back & he agreed to furnish me w/a bus ticket back home if I did just come & try. So I came. . . .

Love, Janis

Big Brother and the Holding
Company at the Palace of Fine Arts,
San Francisco. © Baron Wolman

Woodstock

by John Byrne Cooke

Monterey was an event; Woodstock was a phenomenon. The two years between these gatherings saw the rise of sixties rock and the mobilization of an audience that went far beyond the hippies and the counterculture and the war protesters and the flower children. Who would have thought that a quarter million of them would find their way to Max Yasgur's farm near White Lake, in Bethel, New York, by VW bugs, Greyhound buses, hitchhiking, and pure luck?

One night, two men were talking in an Irish bar down by the railroad tracks in Berkeley, California. One a biker in his thirties, the other an accountant in his twenties. "Let's go to Woodstock," one said. An hour later they were on the bike and on the road. From across the country, the trickles and streams coalesced into a flood that was christened Woodstock Nation. The crowd withstood the mud and the reeking port-a-potties and the bad trips and the delays between sets and the interminable announcements — *"Laura Smith, Bobo is freaking out. Please come to the Good Karma refreshment stand"*—and everything. For the handful who had been at Monterey, it summoned up the afterglow, despite the quantum jump in scale.

Like Monterey, Woodstock was a turning point, but this time it was not for the better. It was so much more than anyone had anticipated that nothing that followed it could match it or surprise us, and we lost our sense of wonder. The makeup of the audiences was changing too. It was the difference between fans who had discovered the music on their own and those who were attracted to it only after reading about rock festivals and the attendant hippie flower-child peacemarcher dopesmoker dropout free-love lifestyle in *Time* and *Newsweek* and *Rolling Stone* (which was first published that year). Rock concerts weren't celebrations of the counterculture anymore. They had joined the mainstream.

For Janis, the changing nature of the audience meant new problems. Increasingly she found their expectations in direct conflict with her own. Nothing was more important to her than getting an honest response from the crowd, setting up communication in which she and they were equal partners. If the communication was right and if there was a little magic in the air, they'd both get off. But the kids now came expecting to get off every time, and they no longer took responsibility for helping to make it happen. They wanted it done *to* them. They demanded it. Janis and the audience were each looking for a different kind of magic, and this difference often made it impossible for either to be satisfied.

August 22, 1966

Mother . . .

. . . First of all, we begin a 4 week engagement in Chicago next Tuesday — at $1000 a week!! So don't write till you hear from me. Really looking forward to going . . . . Chicago is Blues HEAVEN & I can hear & be heard by some important people. They (the club we're playing in — Mother Blues) pay our transportation, so we're flying out Tue. morning. I really dig flying — & being a R&R band & flying to a gig is even more exciting. SIGH!! And a friend of mine gave me a dress & cape to wear for the occasion — a wine-colored velvet, old, from a Goodwill store, but beautiful! Queen Anne kind of sleeves & a very low & broad neckline. Really fantastic. . . .

JANIS

Monterey International Pop
Festival, Fairgrounds, Monterey,
California, Jun. 16–18, 1967
Other performers: The Mamas &
the Papas, Jefferson Airplane,
the Grateful Dead, Otis
Redding, Country Joe and the
Fish, Lou Rawls, The Who, the
Jimi Hendrix Experience, Simon
and Garfunkel, Ravi Shankar,
and War, Booker T. and the
MG's, Canned Heat, Hugh
Masekela, The Association,
Beverly, the Blues Project,
Buffalo Springfield, Paul
Butterfield Blues Band, Electric
Flag, Steve Miller Blues Band,
Moby Grape, The Paupers,
Quicksilver Messenger Service,
Johnny Rivers

15

16

17

Big Brother, with Steve Miller
Blues Band, Sandy Bull, Dan
Hicks, and Santana, Matrix
Benefit, Fillmore,
San Francisco, 1968

Kozmic Blues Band records
I Got Dem 'Ol Kozmic Blues
Again, Mama, Los Angeles,
Jun. 16–26, 1969

18

Big Brother, Red Dog Saloon,
Virginia City, Nevada,
Jun. 17 & 18, 1966

19

Big Brother, Tim Leary Benefit,
St. Francis Hotel, San
Francisco, 1966

Full Tilt, College Park,
Maryland, Jun. 19 & 20, 1970

20

Big Brother, with Grateful Dead
and Quicksilver Messenger
Service, Summer Solstice
Celebration, Golden Gate Park,
San Francisco, 1967

21

22 Big Brother, Carousel Ballroom, San Francisco, Jun. 22 & 23, 1968

23 Big Brother, with Quicksilver Messenger Service, Avalon Ballroom, San Francisco, Jun. 24 & 25, 1966

24 Big Brother, with the Peanut Butter Conspiracy, Debutante Cotillion, Burlingame Country Club, Burlingame, California, 1968

25

Full Tilt, Schenectady, New York, 1970

26 Big Brother, with Quicksilver Messenger Service, Avalon Ballroom, 1967

Big Brother, Denver, Jun. 28 & 29, 1968

27 Full Tilt, Festival Express first concert, Toronto, 1970; other performers on this three-concert train tour: The Band, the Grateful Dead, Delaney and Bonnie and Friends, Ian and Sylvia, New Riders of the Purple Sage, Tom Rush, Buddy Guy, Eric Andersen, Mountain, Ten Years After, Traffic, Seatrain, Charlebois, James & the Good Brothers, Cat, Mashmakan, and the Modern Rock Quartet

28

June

29

Kozmic Blues,
St. Louis, 1969

30

This page *Festival Express
performer passes*

Opposite page: *Festival Express
program*

June

FESTIVAL
EXPRESS
1970

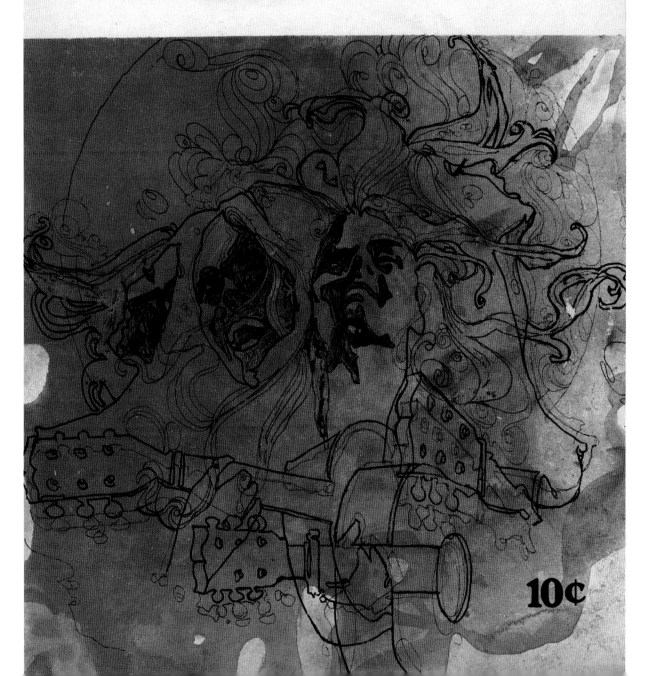

10¢

"**Y**ou never can tell. . . . Sometimes they think they're gonna like you. And then you get out there and you really damage and offend their femininity. You know, 'No chick is supposed to stand like that.' I mean, crouching down in front of the guitar player goin' 'uuuuhhhn!' You know, lettin' your tits shake around, and your hair's stringy, you have no makeup on, and sweat running down your face, you're coming up to the fuckin' microphone, man, and at one point their heads just go 'click,' and they go 'Oooh, no!' You get that a lot. It's really far out. When you're standing on stage you can't see the whole crowd. The trouble is the groovy crowd is usually in the back, because they can't afford the seats down front — the seats down front are the local rich people, the local doctors' sons and their country club dates. They're the ones that are just sitting there, man, with their knees just so. You know, only cross at your ankles, keep your panty girdle tight together, and you sit with your hands in your lap. And I'm up there singing, I'm going, 'Cha-cha-boom-quack-quack,' and I look out at the crowd and the front rows are goin' — these girls have these little pinched smiles and the expressions on their faces are of absolute horror. They've never seen anything like it, and they don't want to again, man. The chick's up there, shakin' it all and sayin', 'How do you like that, boys?' and all the boys are goin', 'Aaaaaaghhh!' The girls are going, 'Oh, my God, she may be able to sing, but she doesn't have to act like that!'"

— JANIS

Postcard home, July 3, 1966
© 1992 Fantality Corp.

July 3

HELLO!

In Monterey this weekend for an "Independence Dance." Beautiful country — have a photographer from this Sunday's paper to send for illustration. Work's going fine except a lot of hassles w/ the union (& think I'm going Republican). A letter brimming w/ news as soon as I have time to write. Like to hear from you — Love XX Janis

TO:
THE JOPLIN FAMILY
3130 LOMBARDY
PORT ARTHUR, TEX.

Big Brother and the Holding Company, with Quicksilver Messenger Service and The Jaywalkers, Fillmore Auditorium, San Francisco, 1966

Kozmic Blues Band, Edwardsville, Illinois, 1969

Full Tilt Boogie Band, Festival Express second concert, Winnipeg, Manitoba, 1970

Big Brother, with Quicksilver Messenger Service and the Gladstones, Monterey Fairgrounds, Monterey, California, 1966

Big Brother, Mt. Tamalpais Outdoor Festival, Marin, California, 1967

Kozmic Blues, Des Moines, Iowa, 1969

Big Brother, with Bo Diddley and Big Joe Williams, Fillmore Auditorium, San Francisco, Jul. 4–6, 1967

Full Tilt, Festival Express final concert, Calgary, Alberta, 1970

Big Brother, Concord, California, 1968

Kozmic Blues, Atlanta International Pop Festival, 1969

Full Tilt, Seattle, 1970

Big Brother, Santa Rosa Fairgrounds, Santa Rosa, California, 1968

Full Tilt, Honolulu, 1970

Big Brother, San Carlos Circle Theater, San Carlos, California, Jul. 7 & 8, 1967

Big Brother, Free concert, Golden Gate Park, San Francisco, 1968

1
2
3
4
5
6
7

End of July, Big Brother moves into a house in Lagunitas, which is dubbed "Argentina," 1966

July

Janis's passport. © 1992 Fantality Corp.

Kozmic Blues Band

by John Byrne Cooke

"I got dem ol' kozmic blues again Mama!"

© John Byrne Cooke

It was a band with no name. A suggestion for "Janis and the Joplinaires" got a few laughs, but it sounded like a fifties doo-wop group and this band was . . . something else. It was put together by musician-consultants that Albert Grossman trusted and it was no family band. The seven musicians were from disparate backgrounds, both personal and musical. Sam Andrew came from Big Brother to play guitar. He was a link to the past, a kindred soul, brought along because Janis couldn't bear to leave him behind. The horn section reflected Janis's love of the Motown sound. Beyond that nod to the black roots of soul music, neither Janis nor anyone else knew what the band might become.

The rock press, furious with Janis for abandoning Big Brother, greeted the new band with malicious reviews as the band struggled to find a musical identity. Onstage, the music was sometimes ragged, but not all the bad reviews were deserved. Sometimes the music found its stride, and the figure at the microphone was still Janis.

© John Byrne Cooke

A European tour in the spring of 1969 was a triumph. For a brief shining moment it all came together. Far from the hostility of the American press, the European audiences had no loyalties to Big Brother and the Holding Company. They wanted to hear Janis Joplin and they heard her at her best. In Frankfurt, a crowd heavily seeded with U.S. military personnel mobbed the stage to Janis's delight. In London's Albert Hall, the staid British audience jumped to its feet and danced. The demonstration was unprecedented. On to Stockholm, Amsterdam, Copenhagen, and Paris.

Back in the U.S.A., the band rode for a time on the European high, but ultimately failed to find a cohesive musical personality. Janis didn't know what kind of sound she really wanted. She let Sam go at last and brought in a new guitar player, but the problems remained. Janis wrote a song with her new record producer that expressed her frustration. She dubbed it "Kozmic Blues," and the band became the Kozmic Blues Band, but the band, like the song, was destined to symbolize for Janis the pain of failed dreams.

Janis's ASCAP cards, 1968, 1969, 1970.

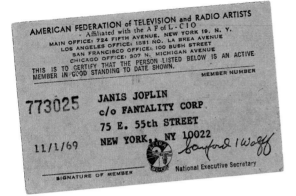

Janis's Union Card, 1969

July

15

Big Brother, with Love, Avalon Ballroom, San Francisco, Jul. 15 & 16, 1966

16

Big Brother, with Richie Havens and Illinois Speed Press, Fillmore–Carousel, San Francisco, Jul. 16–18, 1968

Kozmic Blues, taping of "The Dick Cavett Show," 1969

17

Full Tilt, Albuquerque, New Mexico, 1970

18

19

Kozmic Blues, Forest Hills Tennis Stadium, Queens, New York, 1969

20

Big Brother, with Mount Rushmore, Canned Heat, and Mother Earth, Avalon Ballroom, San Francisco, Jul. 20–22, 1967

Big Brother, Salt Lake City, 1968

21

Big Brother, Westbury Music
Fair, Long Island, 1968

22

Big Brother, with the Grateful
Dead, Straight Theater,
San Francisco, 1967

23

24

Big Brother, Columbia
Records Convention,
Puerto Rico, 1968

25

Kozmic Blues, Post Pavilion,
Maryland, July 25 & 26,
1969

26

Big Brother, Newport Folk
Festival, Newport,
Rhode Island, 1968

27

Big Brother, with the Great
Society and the Charlatans,
Bilbo's Birthday, California
Hall, San Francisco, 1966

28

Big Brother, with the
Charlatans, California Hall,
San Francisco,
July 28–30, 1967

July

"Janis Joplin sings the blues as hard as any black person." Said B.B. King.  "It's about the war between the sexes."

29

30

31

"Janis Joplin's talent was that you believed she was singing her guts out every night."

— Bill Graham

Becoming Pearl

by John Byrne Cooke

In the spring of 1970, Janis set out to put together a new band. No horn section this time. No musicians chosen by others who were unsure what she needed or what she wanted. This time the mistakes—or the triumph—would be hers. Brad Campbell and John Till, survivors of the Kozmic Blues, were living in San Francisco on retainer, biding their time. Albert Grossman brought Richard Bell on piano and Ken Pearson on organ down from Canada for Janis's approval. She approved. Brad and John were playing at a topless joint in San Francisco. The drummer was Clark Pierson, an American version of Ringo Starr with the same happy-go-lucky basic rhythm.

Want to go on the road, Clark? Sure.

The new band was complete, but first it needed a name. Enter Bob Neuwirth, former road manager for Bob Dylan, friend and confidant to Albert Grossman, painter, picker, singer, and sometime songwriter. Dropping by a rehearsal, recruiting companions for an evening's carousal, he demanded, "Is everybody ready for a full tilt boogie?" "Full Tilt Boogie!" Janis shouted, and the Full Tilt Boogie Band was born.

Janis confided to the boys in the band that she wanted a personal nickname, something that suggested a good-time woman, like "Rose," or "Pearl." After a little discussion it came down to these two. Janis decided that "Rose" didn't sound right, so "Pearl" she became, the name already taking on an identity separate from the public persona of Janis Joplin. It was a way for her to appear among her friends as a peer—not a star. It was a private name, an intimate name, used for saying friendly things. We'd say, "Knock 'em dead, Pearl" before a show, or "You're lookin' good, Pearl!" or "Hey, sit down and tell me what's wrong, Pearl," or "Good night, Pearl," but when the talk was about business, or when communications got strained, as they do on the road, it was always Janis then, never Pearl. Pearl was reserved for the close times. It was a name that told her we loved her.

1

Columbia Records releases Big Brother and the Holding Company's Cheap Thrills album, which goes on to top the charts, 1968

2

Big Brother and the Holding Company, with Jefferson Airplane, Losers South, San Jose, Aug. 2–4, 1966

Big Brother, with the Staple Singers and Ten Years After, Fillmore East, New York City, Aug. 2 & 3, 1968

3

Full Tilt Boogie Band, Forest Hills Tennis Stadium, New York City, 1970 (the original date, Aug. 1, was rained out)

Kozmic Blues Band, Atlantic City, 1969

Full Tilt, taping of "The Dick Cavett Show," 1970

4

Big Brother, Avalon Ballroom, San Francisco, 1966

Full Tilt, Ravinia Park, Highland Park, Illinois, 1970

5

Full Tilt, Peace Festival, Shea Stadium, New York City, 1970

6

Big Brother, with Quicksilver Messenger Service, the Grateful Dead, Grassroots, Sunshine, The Committee, the San Francisco Mime Troupe, the Jook Savages, and PH Factor, Benefit for Children's Adventure Day Camp, Fillmore Auditorium, San Francisco, 1966

7

August

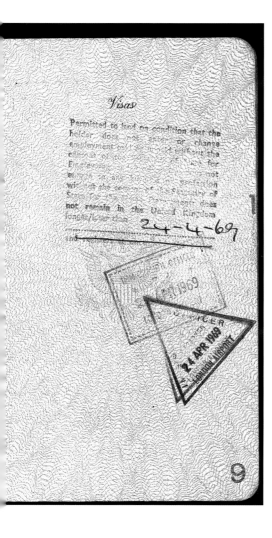

Kozmic Blues, Woodstock
Music & Art Fair, Bethel, New
York, Aug. 16, 1969
Other performers on the 16th:
Canned Heat, Creedence
Clearwater Revival, the
Grateful Dead, Keef Hartley,
Jefferson Airplane, Mountain,
Quill, Santana, The Who

Janis attends her ten-year
high school reunion, Port
Arthur, Texas, 1970

Big Brother, Cheetah,
Chicago, 1968

Big Brother, Tyrone Guthrie
Theater, Minneapolis, 1968

15

16

17

18

19

20

21

Welcome to the Newport Folk Festival!

On your arrival you will be given passes for yourself and your family.
Please DO NOT LOSE these passes or allow any other person to use them.
You will need them to be admitted to the field and to be fed. You will
also be given a room assignment. If you are staying in Vernon Court,
we would like to ask your help. There are many performers staying in
the dorms, and if you would hang your towels over the foot of your bed
rather than in the bathroom, it would simplify the work for our chamber-
maids. Please stay in the room assigned to you. You may see empty beds,
but they are all reserved for performers arriving later. All the blankets,
pillows and linen are the property of Vernon Court Junior College.
Please do not remove this property from the premises. If you have any
question about your accommodations, please see Mrs. von Schmidt or Mrs.
St. Louis at Walsh House (846-5500 Extension 72)

Meals will be served at Walsh House. On performing days, lunch will be
served from a tent at the back of the field.

BREAKFAST	8 a.m. to 10:00 a.m.
LUNCH	12:30 to 2:00 p.m.
DINNER	5:30 to 7:00 p.m.

On Friday and Saturday, lunch will be served at the field for all
performers. Lunch for those performing on Wednesday daytime will be at
the field. Others may eat at Walsh.

There will be a transportation center at the field on the porch of the
performers' building. If you need a ride, please go there and wait
there until the car arrives. There will be someone there with first
aid and emergency supplies as well, so if you have any problem on the
field, the person there can help you.

The transportation from the houses will be handled through Mrs. St.
Louis and Mrs. von Schmidt, at Walsh House.

Please call on us if you have any question or problem. We would like
to make you as comfortable as possible during your stay at the Festival.

The Newport Folk Festival

Janis in the audience at the Newport Folk Festival, 1968. © Elliott Landy, LandyVision, Inc.
Left:*Accommodations instruction sheet given to performers at the Newport Folk Festival.*

Newport Folk Festival logo

Full Tilt Boogie Band

by John Byrne Cooke

The Full Tilt Boogie Band's first concerts were judiciously planned for out-of-the-way cities where any rough spots in the music could be ironed out, but this caution proved unnecessary. The music was jubilant, and the concerts went well. Janis and the band grew closer in the first weeks of its tour than she had ever become in a year with the Kozmic Blues Band. She was the undisputed leader of the new band but she didn't flaunt her authority. She had a confident understanding of the aspects of her business that had eluded her before. The fear of failure, the edge of desperation that had lingered throughout the Kozmic Blues year was gone. Confident in her group, her music, and her songs, Janis recaptured her audience without a fight. By the time she and Full Tilt boarded a chartered train in June 1970 for a whistle-stop tour of huge rock concerts in Canada, she knew she had a winner.

The Festival Express train trip was the high point of the summer tour, carrying 150 musicians and road crew from Toronto to Winnepeg and on to Calgary on the high western plains. It was a stellar lineup: Janis Joplin, the Grateful Dead, The Band, Delaney and Bonnie and Friends, Tom Rush, the

Buddy Guy Blues Band, Ian and Sylvia, Mountain, Traffic, Seatrain, and more. Within hours of boarding the train after the Toronto concert, the musicians discovered that the two bar cars sported 110-volt AC outlets along both walls. Equipment men were dispatched to the baggage cars for amps and microphones. For five days, it was a nonstop picking party.

After the raucous train tour across Canada, Janis and the Full Tilt Boogie Band played in Seattle, then Honolulu, where they took a few days off for badly needed rest. Janis left the boys on the beach at Waikiki while she flew

Janis with Ken Pierson (left), keyboard player for Full Tilt Boogie Band and Brad Campbell (right) bass player for Kosmic Blues Band; in a park in Ohio at a local radio station live broadcast at an Arts and Crafts festival. 1970.

to Austin, Texas, to appear at a seventieth birthday party for Ken Threadgill, who had given Janis her first singing job eight years earlier in his small club. Janis's appearance at the party was a complete surprise. The secret was kept at her insistence, not because she wanted to make a splashy entrance but because she didn't want to steal the spotlight from a man she loved and admired. She played the guitar and sang two songs for him. The rest of the time she was just another celebrant, enjoying the party and reminiscing with a few friends from her early days in Austin when she was first singing the blues.

In August, Janis went back to Texas again, this time to her home town of Port Arthur, for her ten-year high school reunion. She explained her reasons for making this trip on a "Dick Cavett Show" that aired before the event: "Honey, they laughed me out of class, out of town, and out of the state. Now I'm going home." In Port Arthur, Janis wore her most outrageous outfits and gloried in the attention she got. She had a much better time than her classmates. Except for one relaxed young couple—local hippies who took their smiling baby to all the reunion events—Janis's contemporaries in Port Arthur didn't seem to have any fun at all. Janis got a prize for having come the longest distance to get there: they gave her a bald tire.

Extended family of the Family Dog in San Francisco - Chet Helms, center, top of van; Janis in dark glasses 6th from right sourrounded by Big Brother Band members. © Herb Greene

June 1966

. . . Still working w/ Big Brother & the Holding Co. & it's really fun! Four guys in the group— Sam, Peter, Dave, & James. We rehearse every afternoon in a garage that's part of a loft an artist friend of theirs owns & people constantly drop in and listen — everyone seems very taken w/ my singing although I am a little dated. This kind of music is differ-ent than I'm used to. Oh, I've collected more bizarre names of groups to send — (can you believe these?!) The Grateful Dead, The Love, Jefferson Airplane, Quicksilver Messenger Service, The Leaves, The Grass Roots.

 Chet Helms heads a rock & roll corporation called the Family Dog — replete w/ emblem & answering service. Very fancy. Being my entrepreneur (and mostly having gotten me out here without money — I still have $30 in the bank I'm hoarding) Chet rented me this place for a month. He says if the band & I don't make it, to forget it & if we do, we'll have plenty of money. Chet is an old friend — married now to an actress named Lori. Tomorrow night at his dance, some people from Mercury will be there to hear the Grateful Dead (with a name like that, they have to be good . . .) and Big Brother et. al. and I'm going to get to sing! Gosh I'm so excited! We've worked out about 5 or 6 numbers this week —one I really like called "Down on Me" — an old spiritual — revitalized and slightly bastardized w/ new treatment.

 I'm still okay —don't worry. Something of a recluse. Haven't lost or gained any weight & my head's still fine. And am still really *thinking of coming back to school, so don't give up on me yet. I love you all*

XXXX

Janis

Big Brother signs with
Mainstream Records, 1966

22

Big Brother begins four-week
gig at Mother Blues Club,
Chicago, 1966

Big Brother, Singer Bowl,
Queens, New York City, 1968

23

Kozmic Blues, Convention
Hall, Asbury Park, New Jersey,
1969

Big Brother, with Bo Diddley,
Bukka White, and the
Salvation Army Banned,
Avalon Ballroom, San
Francisco, Aug. 24–27, 1967

24

25

26

Kozmic Blues, Saratoga
Performing Arts Camp,
Saratoga Springs,
New York, 1969

27

28

August

© Gene Anthony.

1970 Janis came to Taos New Mexico with Manager Al Grossman, to do a cigar commercial on the Rio Grande Gorge Bridge. Tom and I went to meet them at the LaFonda Hotel. Janis whispered in my ear "you can help me, help me!" I thought, at last I can do something to help Janis, she always seems so troubled. **"I'm tired of these city men I want me a mountain man."** This photo was taken at 1 p.m. after she found her mountain man who lived in a small adobe house at the foot of the Sangre De Cristo Mountains in the Pentente village of Truchas.

—Lisa Law

Janis in Truchas   Lisa Law

Big Brother, Straight Theater,
San Francisco,
Sept. 1–3, 1967

1

*Big Brother and the Holding Company records
their first Mainstream album, Fall 1966*

*Columbia releases I Got Dem 'Ol Kozmic Blues
Again, Mama, 1969*

*Full Tilt Boogie Band records the Pearl album,
Los Angeles, 1970*

2

3

Big Brother, Debutante party,
La Dolphine Estate, 1967

4

5

Big Brother, with Iron Butterfly
and the Fraternity of Man,
Hollywood Bowl, 1968

6

7

September

" 'Why is everyone a pair except me?' Janis wondered. 'I want to want the white house with the picket fence covered with climbing roses, but I just don't,' she often said with a sigh."
— Laura Joplin, from *Love, Janis*

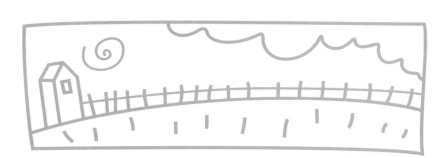

8

Big Brother, with Blue Cheer, 1601 West Evans Street, Denver, Sept. 8 & 9, 1967

Kozmic Blues Band, taping of "Music Scene" television show, Los Angeles, 1969

9

10

11

Big Brother, with Santana and Chicago Transit Authority, Fillmore West, San Francisco, Sept. 12–14, 1968

12

13

14

 Big Brother, Hollywood Bowl, 1967

Big Brother, Monterey Jazz Festival, Monterey, California, Sept. 15–17, 1967

Big Brother, with Joan Baez, the Everly Brothers, The Byrds, Country Joe and the Fish, Junior Wells, Buddy Guy, the Mothers of Invention, Buffy St. Marie, and Wilson Pickett, Rose Bowl, Pasadena, 1968

Kozmic Blues, rehearsal for "This Is Tom Jones" television show, Los Angeles, 1969

Kozmic Blues, Hollywood Bowl, 1969

Kozmic Blues, taping of "This Is Tom Jones," 1969

15

16

17

18

19

20

21

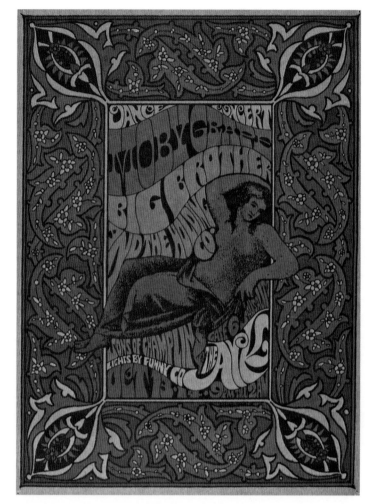

Moby Grape; Big Brother and the Holding Company, The Ark, Sausalito, 1967

September

© Gene Anthony.

22

23 Big Brother, with Howlin' Wolf,
Avalon Ballroom, San Francisco,
Sept. 23 & 24, 1966

24

25

26

27 Big Brother, University of
California, Irvine, 1968

28 Big Brother, San Diego, 1968

Cry Baby, Cry Baby, Baby,

Honey, welcome back home.
I know she told you, Honey I
know she told you
that she loved you much
more then I, yeah;
all I know is that she left
you and you swear that you
just don't know why,
But you know, honey, always,
I'll be around if you ever
want me. Come on and Cry,
Cry, Baby, Cry,
Baby, Cry, Baby.

CRY BABY
Words and Music by Bert Russell and
Norman Meade © 1963 EMI PUBLISHING LTD. and
UNICHAPPELL MUSIC INC.

© Gene Anthony.

Busted flat in Baton Rouge,

Headin' for the trains; Feelin' nearly faded as my jeans, Bobby thumbed a diesel down just before it rained; Took us all the way to New Orleans.

—from *Me and Bobby McGee*
Words and Music by Kris
Kristofferson and Fred Foster
© 1969 TEMI COMBINE INC.

Janis and Kris Kristofferson in Los Angeles, 1970. © Clark Pierson

29 Big Brother, taping of "Hollywood Palace" television show, Los Angeles, 1968

30

August 13, 1966

Dear Family . . .

At last a tranquil day & time to write all the good news. I am now safely moved into my new room in our beautiful house in the country. I'm the only member of the band out here so far. Our landlady & one of her daughters are still here but they've gone out to dinner so I'm all alone, sitting in a comfortable chair by the fireplace, doors wide open and a 180° view of trees, redwood & fir. Bliss! I've never felt so relaxed in my life. This is the most fantastic house & setting. I really wish you could see it. Of course part of my comfort is due to the fact that this is the first day in 10 or 11 that I've had to relax at all. We've been working every night for 11 days. S.F., Vancouver, S.F. again –– and we really worked! Last night, for example, we played a benefit. They had scads of talent –– 5 rock bands, 2 poets, 2 comedians, a puppet show, etc. Went on from 3 pm to 1 am. We went on at 5 and again at midnight. Really was exciting though . . . two of the bands have hit records out –– the Grass Roots (who incidentally are big fans of ours and even wear *our* buttons when they play) and the Jefferson Airplane –– and were very well received, but I/we got an ovation, bigger than any other groups, for a slow blues in a minor key. Wow, I can't help it –– I love it! People really treat me with deference. I'm somebody important. SIGH!! . . .

There's such an upsurge among teenagers trying/wanting to be hip. Several of my friends own dress shops & make really far-out clothes for them, others make beads & sell them, others make leather things, but most of them are in the rock & roll business. Really fantastic –– a social phenomena really. The society seems to be leaning away from itself, straining for the periphery of hell, the edges, you know. At least in California. Now *that is* a qualifying statement. . . .

Oh this weekend . . . . we're playing at the Avalon. . . . But some good friends, the Grateful Dead are playing there –– they're also neighbors, one of the 2 other groups that live out here. Just down the road a piece. . . .

XXX

Janis

"Janis came into the dressing room at the Fillmore East, she had this rabbit fur purse on her shoulder and she had her pint of Southern Comfort in it. She offered me a swig, said it made her sing better. I said, 'I can't take a swig now Janis, it might blow my pipes!' She asked me to sing a gospel song with her, so we sang 'Down by the Riverside.' The crowd went wild. That was the last time we saw Janis."

— Mavis Staples, The Staple Singers

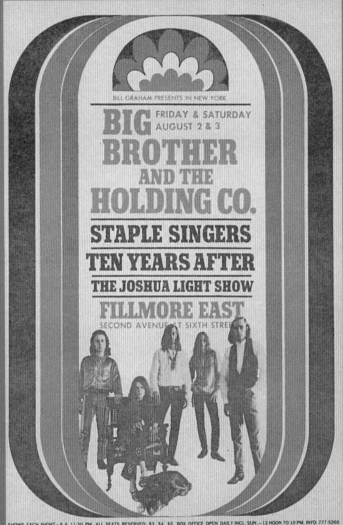

Handbill, for Big Brother and the Holding Company;
Staple Singers. Fillmore East, New York, 1968
© *Bill Graham Presents*

Paul and Janis

by John Byrne Cooke

Paul Rothchild had an uncanny ability to express musical concepts and suggestions in words. He did it so effectively that The Doors, the Paul Butterfield Blues Band, and a host of folk singers produced definitive albums under his guidance. Albert Grossman hoped Paul's talents would allow him to connect with Janis in a way that her previous record producers had failed to do.

Paul admired Janis's music. He thought she was even better than either she or the world yet suspected, and he wanted to draw out the truly great singer he was convinced she was and get her on tape for the first time. But to do that, they'd have to hit it off.

Janis's road manager, John Cooke, was an old friend of Paul's. In July, 1970 he brought them together on the deck of Janis's new home in Marin County, California, where they sat in sunlight filtered through the redwoods. Janis smoothed over the first awkward moments with a pitcher of piña coladas. They talked and drank the day away. Janis revealed her humor and her intelligence, and Paul knew that he could work with her.

Paul and Janis became friends. As they worked together, Paul became one of a handful of intimates with whom Janis would reveal herself. One evening over drinks, he said to her:

"Come on, Pearl, what do you really sing like?" And she said "I'll show you." And she sang me stuff out of the church choir. And I heard this pure, straight, white voice. Clean, clear, no vibrato, no fur, no broken glass and rusty razor blades, just "Ahhhh," soprano. And I said "Right, you can sing. Fantastic." I was pointing out to her that that voice was her salvation and it was toward that voice that she had to evolve

Janis with producer Paul Rothchild.
© Clark Pierson.

her next voice. You know, a good singer's voice goes through evolution and develops. They all do. And she should start working toward a pure sound. Because she couldn't do "Ball and Chain" Janis Joplin at age forty. It would be ludicrous. And she loved this because it was talk about real direction, what she should do with her vocal career and her future, and what to aim for, and she was going for it.

When Janis died, Paul mourned her with as much feeling as the friends who had known her for years. Looking back on their relationship, he said, "Of all the lead singers that I know or have worked with, she was the most workable singer. I mean she was a producer's dream, for me. Whatever the reasons, it was a perfect union."

Seth

by John Byrne Cooke

There was another man in Janis's life that summer who saw her working toward the woman she could become. Seth Morgan was a rich kid hiding his origins under a biker-punk veneer. Janis loved the punk, and the inner man as well. When they had run through the drinking and the brag talk, they discovered the comfort of quiet times together when they talked of books and ideas and the world at large. They talked of marriage, too.

Seth came to Los Angeles on weekends while Janis and the Full Tilt Boogie boys were recording with Paul. During the week he hit the books in Berkeley, trying for an overdue degree. He didn't belong to the music world, didn't feel at home in the studio or hanging out with the band. He knew Janis was courting danger in her off-hours, trying to quell boredom by flirting with old destructive habits she had kicked out of her life back in the spring. She begged him to make her stop and he told her only she could stop. She promised she would when the *Pearl* record was done.

But Janis tripped and fell, struck down by a dealer's forgetfulness, by uncut heroin that killed several others in that fatal week. Seth Morgan saw the tragedy of her accidental death for what it was, and put it in perspective:

> *She was concentrating more on herself, and building herself. I think I was a*
> *very important part of that, but had I not been there I think that a pattern*
> *was beginning to develop that would have gone on. I think it was inexorable.*
> *. . . I feel that she was coming into her own, emotionally, as a person, and*
> *that the drug use was so incidental, that her death was such a filthy, dirty*
> *little trick.*

October

1 Kozmic Blues Band, Tempe, Arizona, 1969

2 Big Brother, Cleveland, 1968

Kozmic Blues, San Diego Sports Arena, San Diego, 1969

3 Janis dies of an accidental overdose of heroin in Los Angeles, 1970. The *Pearl* album is completed after her death by producer Paul Rothchild and the Full Tilt Boogie Band. It goes to #1 for nine weeks and contains a hit single, Janis's version of Kris Kristofferson's "Me and Bobby McGee."

4 Big Brother, State University of New York, Buffalo, 1968

Kozmic Blues, Winterland, San Francisco, 1969

5 Big Brother and the Holding Company, Golden Gate Park, San Francisco, 1966

Big Brother, The Matrix, San Francisco, 1967

6 Big Brother, with Jack & the Ripper, The Ark, Sausalito, California, 1967

7 Big Brother, with Jim Kweskin Jug Band and the Electric Train, Avalon Ballroom, San Francisco, Oct. 7 & 8, 1966

Big Brother, Avalon Ballroom, San Francisco, Oct. 7 & 8, 1967

Big Brother, Haight-Ashbury
Medical Clinic Benefit,
San Jose, 1967

8

9

10

Big Brother, War Memorial
Auditorium, Syracuse,
New York, 1968

11

Kozmic Blues, Sacramento,
1969

12

Big Brother, with Moby
Grape, The Ark, Sausalito,
California, Oct. 13 & 14,
1967

13

Big Brother, Music Hall,
Cincinnati, 1968

October

14

When I first came to
America I played the
Fillmore East with Big
Brother and the Holding
Company and the Staple
Singers. Janis was
passing around her
Southern Comfort, I
had a sip and it seemed
like nice sweet stuff,
so I had some more, and
some more. Later on they
found me, passed out cold
Backstage.

—Alvin Lee,
Ten Years After

15 Big Brother, with the Sir Douglas Quintet, Family Dog one-year anniversary, Avalon Ballroom, San Francisco, Oct. 15 & 16, 1966

16 Big Brother, Avalon Ballroom, San Francisco, Oct. 15 & 16, 1967

Big Brother, Grande Ballroom, Detroit, 1968

17 Kozmic Blues, University of Texas, Austin, 1969

18 Big Brother, Pennsylvania State University, University Park, 1968

Kozmic Blues, San Antonio, 1969

19 Big Brother, Spectrum, Philadelphia, 1968

Kozmic Blues, Houston, 1969

20 Big Brother, Alexandria Roller Rink, Alexandria, Virginia, 1968

21

"She's here tonight, man, you know what I mean? She's in everybody's hearts, mouths, and heads. Everybody says, 'I wish she's here.' She's in my heart, man, screaming . . . laughing . . . bitching, man, bitching."

—Saxophonist Martin Fierro, playing with Quicksilver on the night Janis died.

October

22

23

Big Brother, with the Grateful Dead, Winterland, San Francisco, 1966

24

25

Big Brother, Curry Hicks Cage, University of Massachusetts, Amherst, 1968

26

Big Brother, Worcester Polytechnic Institute, Worcester, Massachusetts, 1968

27

28

Big Brother, Peacock Country Club, San Rafael, California, Oct. 28 & 29, 1967

...DRINKS ARE ON PEARL...

AT THE LION'S SHARE

60 RED HILL ROAD ... SAN ANSELMO

MONDAY, OCTOBER 26TH ... 8:30 P.M.

Invitation to the party Janis had arranged to take place after her death.
She left instructions in her will for $2500 to be set aside for a party
for her friends. © Baron Wolman

29

30

31

Kozmic Blues, Convention
Hall, Philadelphia, 1969

Big Brother signed the contract with Albert
on November 11, 1967. "Janis and I called
him Uncle Albert, " recalled Linda
Gravenites. . . . With genuine affection,
Janis cut out the portrait of the man on the
Quaker Oats box and hung it on the kitchen
wall. It looked just like Uncle Albert.

Big Brother, The Matrix, San
Francisco, Nov. 1–6, 1966

Big Brother, Electric Factory,
Philadelphia, Nov. 1 & 2,
1968

Big Brother, with Pink Floyd
and Richie Havens, Fillmore/
Winterland, San Francisco,
Nov. 2–4, 1967

Big Brother, with Moby Grape,
The Ark, Sausalito,
California, 1967

1

Big Brother and the Holding Company signs
with manager Albert Grossman, 1967

Big Brother's *Cheap Thrills* album hits #1
in Billboard's Top 100, 1968

2

3

4

5

6

7

November

Big Brother band members signing the Columbia Record deal, November 11, 1967.
© John Byrne Cooke

Big Brother, Hunter College,
New York City, 1968

15

Big Brother, State University
of New York, Stony Brook,
1968

16

Kozmic Blues, Tampa,
Florida, 1969

17

18

Big Brother, The Barn, Scott's
Valley, California, 1966

19

20

November

Kozmic Blues, Dane County
Exposition Center, Madison,
Wisconsin, 1969

21

"Once you jump on the floor and start dancin' with them, unless they're sound asleep, *that usually gets 'em up. There's somethin' really strange I've noticed, there's some kind of artificial barrier built into their minds between stage and us* — that's *the stage,* that's *the show. It's like an invisible wall between stage and audience. Once you break that barrier, and you jump down and walk out and touch 'em, and say, 'I'll dance with you, man, I'll get sweaty with you. Come on, I'm with* you, *man . . .' In fact,* I *just happen to be standing on stage. Once they feel that barrier is down, that they're there with you it just rocks right on out, man. It's fun, it's fun. I used to get such a rush from that* contact, *man, and, as a matter of fact I still do. You* gotta *get yourself off first for them to get into it. You gotta love it cause that's the only reason to be doin' it."*

— JANIS

22

Big Brother, with Friendly Stranger, California Hall, San Francisco, Nov. 23 & 24, 1967

23

Big Brother, Houston Music Hall, Houston, 1968

Kozmic Blues, Auditorium Theater, Chicago, 1969

24

Big Brother, Coliseum, Dallas, 1968

Big Brother, with Country Joe and the Fish and Quicksilver Messenger Service, Avalon Ballroom, San Francisco, Nov. 25 & 26, 1966

25

Big Brother, with Mount Rushmore, Avalon Ballroom, San Francisco, 1967

26

Big Brother, Denver Auditorium, Denver, 1968

27

28

Kozmic Blues, Pittsburgh, 1969

November

November 20, 1966

Dear Mother . . . .

. . . had to play for 2 hours straight which is none too easy. The next night into the city
for what ranks as our crowning achievement here-to-fore — a Hell's Angels Party. A
complete madhouse! Then Sunday night we played a zenefit — a benefit for the Zen
Temple here in town. This weekend we played at a place in Santa Cruz called the barn.
It's about 60 mi. away, so we stayed at someone's house & slept on the floor Fri. nite —
which is just barely called resting. Moan. We're at the Avalon Ballroom next week end and
the first part of December we're supposed to be going to L.A. to record. . . .

My car now has Big Brother and the Holding Co. painted on it, and our
symbol, the God's Eye, very good, done by Mouse, one of the poster artists around
did it. Very nice. Car . . . is running well but won't start because of my non-working
starter motor. So I jump-start it rolling down hills. Luckily we live on top of one. . .

—Janis

29
Big Brother, Seattle, 1968

30
Big Brother, Vancouver, 1968

© Jay Good

© Jay Good

Big Brother, Family Dog
Benefit, San Francisco, 1968
— Janis's last gig with
Big Brother

1

Big Brother and the Holding Company plays gigs in Fresno, Turlock, Merced, and other towns in California's San Joaquin Valley, as well as the Golden Bear in Huntington Beach, 1967

Mid-December, Janis and the Kozmic Blues Band perform "Me and Bobby McGee" for the first time in concert, Nashville, 1969

2

3

4

Kozmic Blues, Georgia Tech,
Atlanta, 1969

5

Kozmic Blues, University of
Virginia, Charlottesville, 1969

Broadcast of "This Is Tom
Jones" television show with
Kozmic Blues performance,
1969

6

Janis, with Butterfield Blues
Band and special guest Joe
Cocker, Civic Center, Balti-
more, 1969

7

December

December 1966

Dear Mother . . . .

Just a note to keep you informed. Played a "happening" at Stanford this weekend. It was held in Wilbur Hall, & called—A Happening in the Wilburness. Cute. They had a room featuring sensory awareness, a womb room, a jazz band, an old car that you could wail on w/sledge hammers, & a rock dance. Really fun. . . .

Janis

© Jay Good

Handwritten lyrics in Janis's hand for an unpublished song written by Janis and Dave Getz.

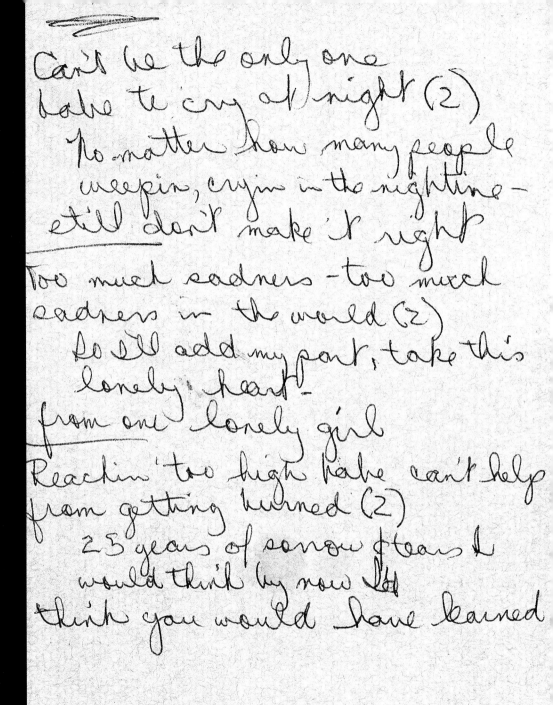

Can't be the only one
babe to cry at night (2)
    No matter how many people
    weepin, cryin in the nighttime—
still don't make it right

Too much sadness - too much
sadness in the world (2)
    So I'll add my part, take this
    lonely heart -
from one lonely girl

Reachin' too high babe can't help
from getting burned (2)
    25 years of sorrow & tears &
    would think by now I'd
think you would have learned

8

9

Big Brother, with Oxford
Circle and Lee Michaels,
Avalon Ballroom, San
Francisco, Dec. 9 & 10, 1966

10

11

12

13

14

December

15

Big Brother, Whiskey-A-Go-Go Los Angeles, Dec. 15 & 16, 1967

16

Big Brother, with Quicksilver Messenger Service, the Loving Impulse, and the Congress of Wonders, Winterland, San Francisco, Dec. 16 & 17, 1966

17

18

19

Kozmic Blues, Madison Square Garden, New York City, 1969 — the last Kozmic Blues Band gig

20

21

Janis's first appearance with her new band, later to be named the Kozmic Blues Band; with the Bar-Kays, Booker T. & the MG's, Albert King, Rufus and Carla Thomas, William Bell, and Eddie Floyd; Stax-Volt Records Christmas Show, Memphis, 1968

22

23

24

First annual Big Brother
Christmas party,
Lagunitas, 1966

25

26

27

28

Big Brother Christmas party,
Sokol Hall,
San Francisco, 1967

December

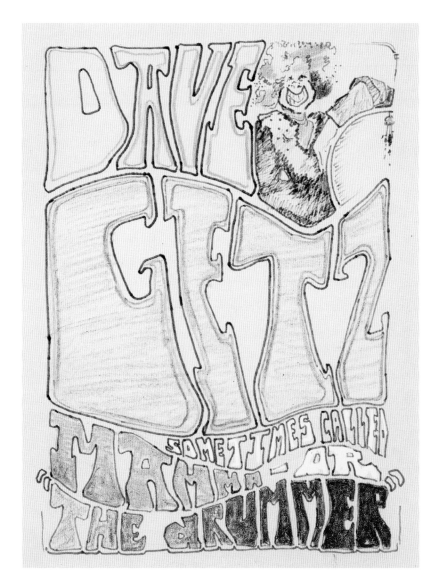

*Janis created handmade Christmas cards
for friends every year. This one was for Dave Getz
and reads: "Dave Getz Sometimes Called Mother
- Or 'The Drummer' 1966.*

29   Big Brother, with Chuck Berry
and Quicksilver Messenger
Service, Fillmore Auditorium,
San Francisco, Dec. 29 & 30,
1967

30

Big Brother, Kezar Pavilion,
Golden Gate Park, San
Francisco, 1966

31   Big Brother, with Jefferson
Airplane and Quicksilver
Messenger Service,
Winterland, San Francisco,
1967

All I know
is something like a bird
within her sang

All I know, she sang a little while
and then flew on

Tell me all that you know
I'll show you
Snow and rain

If you hear that same sweet song again
will you know why?
Anyone who sings a tune so sweet
is passing by

Laugh in the sunshine
sing
cry in the dark
fly through the night

Don't cry now
Don't you cry
Don't you cry
anymore   la-la-la-la

Sleep
in the stars

don't you cry
dry your eyes
on the wind
        la-la-la-la-la . . .

—BIRDSONG, written for Janis,
by Robert Hunter and Jerry Garcia
© copyright Ice Nine Publishing

1-23

Dear Family...

I managed to
pass my - gasp. 27th
birthday without really
feeling it. Not doing
much now - just enjoying
the house. I'm one
month into a supposedly
3 month long vacation
which looks like it
will end up a month &
a half vacation. Sigh.
Ah, such a funny game...
when you're nobody & poor,
you don't care - you can

just drift but when you get a little position & a little money, you start really hustling to get more & then when you're numero uno, you're gotta really freak'ers, so nobody catches you! Catches you?! Two years ago I didn't even want to be it! No, that's not this. I've been looking around & I've noticed something. After you reach a certain level of talent (& quite a few have that talent) the deciding factor is

ambition, or as
I see it, how
much you really need.
Need to be loved ?;
need to be proud of your-
self .... ; I guess thats
what ambition is — it's
not all a degraded quest
for position, Mike, or money,
maybe it's for love. Lots
of love! Ha...

Having some beautiful
work done on the house - the
guys are half artists & half
carpenters — turning a plain
unused, & unexciting wall into
a sunburst of redwood planks
w/ a bar & a set of shelves.

flowing organically
out of both ends —
all rich wood & flowing
shapes. Really defies
description — I'll send
a picture when I'm through.

Linda & I are going to
Rio for Carnival in Feb. Did
you see Black Orpheus? It
took place there — the forefather
of Mardi Gras. The whole
city parties for a week — dancing
in the streets! So we're
going to go....

Got a new little white
dog — Georgi's daughter. If you
ever decide to breed Lady,

(over)

I'd like one of the puppies, we want lots of dogs!!!; Linda has asked specifically for a horse.

My piano teacher just arrived; got to go.

All my love, & thanks for calling!!

Love,

Jan

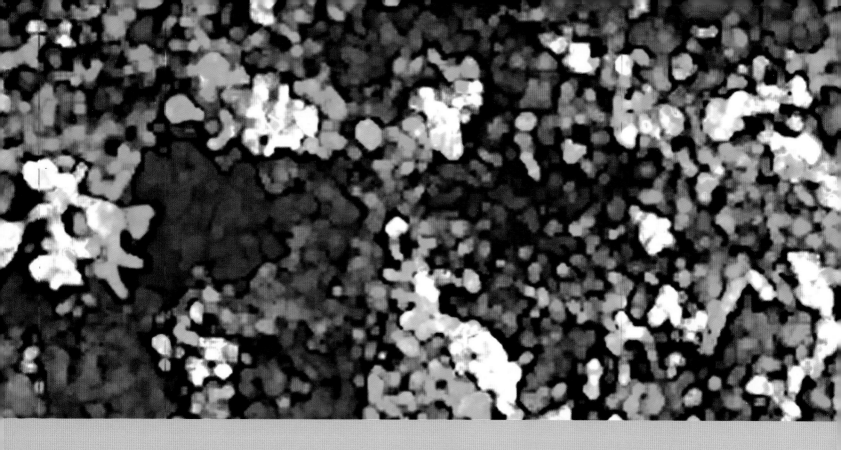

Chronology and Discography

Chronology

January 19, 1943: Janis is born in Port Arthur, Texas.

[1966]

June 1966: Janis moves back to San Francisco from Austin.

June 4, 1966: Janis joins Big Brother and the Holding Company.

June 10, 1966: First performance with Big Brother, Avalon Ballroom, San Francisco.

June 17 & 18, 1966: Big Brother, Red Dog Saloon, Virginia City, Nevada.

June 19, 1966: Big Brother, Tim Leary Benefit, St. Francis Hotel, San Francisco.

June 24 & 25, 1966: Big Brother, with Quicksilver Messenger Service, Avalon Ballroom, San Francisco.

End of July 1966: Big Brother moves into a house in Lagunitas, which is dubbed "Argentina."

July 1, 1966: Big Brother, with Quicksilver Messenger Service and The Jaywalkers, Fillmore Auditorium, San Francisco.

July 2, 1966: Big Brother, with Quicksilver Messenger Service and the Gladstones, Fairgrounds, Monterey, California.

July 14, 1966: Big Brother, with the Grateful Dead and the Hindustani Jazz Sextet, Fillmore Auditorium, San Francisco.

July 15 & 16, 1966: Big Brother, with Love, Avalon Ballroom, San Francisco.

July 28, 1966: Big Brother, with the Great Society and the Charlatans, Bilbo's Birthday, California Hall, San Francisco.

July 29, 1966: Big Brother, Garden Auditorium Trips Festival

August 2–4, 1966: Big Brother and the Holding Company, with Jefferson Airplane, Losers South, San Jose.

August 5, 1966: Big Brother, Avalon Ballroom, San Francisco.

August 7, 1966: Big Brother, with Quicksilver Messenger Service, the Grateful Dead, Grassroots, Sunshine, The Committee, the San Francisco Mime Troupe, the Jook Savages, and PH Factor, Benefit for Children's Adventure Day Camp, Fillmore Auditorium, San Francisco.

August 12 & 13, 1966: Big Brother, with Bo Diddley, Avalon Ballroom, San Francisco.

August 23, 1966: Big Brother signs with Mainstream Records.

August 23, 1966: Big Brother begins a four-week gig at Mother Blues Club, Chicago.

September 23 & 24, 1966: Big Brother, with Howlin' Wolf, Avalon Ballroom, San Francisco.

Fall 1966: Big Brother records their first Mainstream album.

October 6, 1966: Big Brother, Golden Gate Park, San Francisco.

October 7 & 8, 1966: Big Brother, with Jim Kweskin Jug Band and the Electric Train, Avalon Ballroom, San Francisco.

October 15 & 16, 1966: Big Brother, with the Sir Douglas Quintet, Family Dog one-year anniversary, Avalon Ballroom, San Francisco.

October 22, 1966: Big Brother, with the Grateful Dead, Winterland, San Francisco.

November 1–6, 1966: Big Brother, The Matrix, San Francisco.

November 11, 1966: Big Brother, with the Rubber Band, Trip Room, Sacramento.

November 11, 1966: Big Brother, taping of "POW" television show, San Francisco.

November 12, 1966: Big Brother, with the Merry Pranksters, Hells Angels dance, Sokol Hall, San Francisco.

November 19, 1966: Big Brother, The Barn, Scott's Valley, California.

November 25 & 26, 1966: Big Brother, with Country Joe and the Fish and Quicksilver Messenger Service, Avalon Ballroom, San Francisco.

December 9 & 10, 1966: Big Brother, with Oxford Circle and Lee Michaels, Avalon Ballroom, San Francisco.

December 16 & 17, 1966: Big Brother, with Quicksilver Messenger Service, the Loving Impulse, and the Congress of Wonders, Winterland, San Francisco.

December 25, 1966: First annual Big Brother Christmas party, Lagunitas.

December 31, 1966: Big Brother, Kezar Pavilion, Golden Gate Park, San Francisco.

[1967]

January 1967: Big Brother leaves Lagunitas communal house; band members move into individual apartments in the Haight-Ashbury neighborhood, San Francisco.

January 1, 1967: Big Brother, with the Orkustra and the Grateful Dead, New Year's Wail/Whale, Panhandle Park, San Francisco.

January 14, 1967: Big Brother, Human Be-In, Golden Gate Park, San Francisco.

January 15, 1967: Big Brother, with the Merry Pranksters, Shrine Auditorium, Los Angeles .

January 17–22, 1967: Big Brother, The Matrix, San Francisco.

January 29, 1967: Big Brother, with the Grateful Dead, Moby Grape, and Allen Ginsberg, Krishna Temple Benefit, Avalon Ballroom, San Francisco.

February 3, 1967: Big Brother, with Blue Cheer, Hells Angels dance, California Hall, San Francisco.

February 10 & 11, 1967: Big Brother, with Country Joe and the Fish, Golden Sheaf Bakery, Berkeley.

February 17 & 18, 1967: Big Brother, with Quicksilver Messenger Service, Avalon Ballroom, San Francisco.

February 19, 1967: Big Brother, with Jefferson Airplane, Fillmore Auditorium, San Francisco.

February 23, 1967: Big Brother, with the Human Beings, Benefit for the Valley Peace Center, The Ark, Sausalito, California.

March 3, 1967: Big Brother, with Steve Miller, University of California Medical Center, San Francisco.

March 12, 1967: Big Brother, with Country Joe and the Fish, Steve Miller Blues Band, and Quicksilver Messenger Service, Sunflower-Phoenix Dance Benefit for Aid to Vietnam and Mississippi, Fillmore Auditorium, San Francisco.

March 17 & 18, 1967: Big Brother, with Charles Lloyd and the Sir Douglas Quintet, Avalon Ballroom, San Francisco.

March 21–25, 1967: Big Brother, with Citizens for Interplanetary Activities (C.I.A.), The Rock Garden, San Francisco.

March 31 & April 1, 1967: Big Brother, with the Charlatans and Blue Cheer, Avalon Ballroom, San Francisco.

April 11, 1967: Big Brother, Fillmore Auditorium, San Francisco.

April 12 & 13, 1967: Big Brother, Winterland, San Francisco.

April 16, 1967: Big Brother, with the New Breed, Civic Auditorium, Stockton, California.

April 21 & 22, 1967: Big Brother, with Howlin' Wolf, Fillmore Auditorium, San Francisco.

April 23, 1967: Big Brother, with the Charles Lloyd Quartet, California Hall, San Francisco.

April 25–27, 1967: Big Brother, The Matrix, San Francisco.

April 28 & 29, 1967: Big Brother, with Big Mama Thornton, California Hall, San Francisco.

May 5–7, 1967: Big Brother, with the Sir Douglas Quintet and the Orkustra, Avalon Ballroom, San Francisco.

May 11, 1967: Big Brother, with Country Joe and the Fish, Fillmore Auditorium, San Francisco.

May 12 & 13, 1967: Big Brother, Winterland, San Francisco.

May 26 & 27, 1967: Big Brother, with Steve Miller Blues Band, Fillmore Auditorium, San Francisco.

May 30, 1967: Big Brother, with the Jefferson Airplane, Quicksilver Messenger Service, the Charlatans, and the Grateful Dead, Benefit for the Haight-Ashbury Legal Organization, Winterland, San Francisco.

May 31, 1967: Big Brother is filmed as part of the movie "Petulia."

June 2 & 3, 1967: Big Brother, with Country Joe and the Fish and Quicksilver Messenger Service, California Hall, San Francisco.

June 8–11, 1967: Big Brother, with Canned Heat, Avalon Ballroom, San Francisco.

June 16–18, 1967: Big Brother, Monterey International Pop Festival, Fairgrounds, Monterey, California.

June 21, 1967: Big Brother, with the Grateful Dead and Quicksilver Messenger Service, Summer Solstice Celebration, Golden Gate Park, San Francisco.

June 27, 1967: Big Brother, with Quicksilver Messenger Service, Avalon Ballroom.

July 2, 1967: Big Brother, Mt. Tamalpais Outdoor Festival, Marin, California.

July 4–6, 1967: Big Brother, with Bo Diddley and Big Joe Williams, Fillmore Auditorium, San Francisco.

July 7 & 8, 1967: Big Brother, San Carlos Circle Theater, San Carlos, California.

July 14 & 15, 1967: Big Brother, with Quicksilver Messenger Service, Grand Opening of the Continental Ballroom, Santa Clara, California.

July 20–22, 1967: Big Brother, with Mount Rushmore, Canned Heat, and Mother Earth, Avalon Ballroom, San Francisco.

July 23, 1967: Big Brother, with the Grateful Dead, Straight Theater, San Francisco.

July 28–30, 1967: Big Brother, with the Charlatans, California Hall, San Francisco.

July 31, 1967: Big Brother, with Blue Cheer and the Charlatans, Free Clinic Benefit, San Francisco.

August 1967: Big Brother's first album release on Mainstream, Big Brother and the Holding Company.

August 11 & 12, 1967: Big Brother, with the Charles Lloyd Quartet, Continental Ballroom, Santa Clara, California.

August 24–27, 1967: Big Brother, with Bo Diddley, Bukka White, and the Salvation Army Banned, Avalon Ballroom, San Francisco.

September 1–3, 1967: Big Brother, Straight Theater, San Francisco.

September 4, 1967: Big Brother, Dubutante party, La Dolphine Estate, California.

September 8 & 9, 1967: Big Brother, with Blue Cheer, 1601 West Evans Street, Denver.

September 15–17, 1967: Big Brother, Monterey Jazz Festival, Monterey, California.

October 6, 1967: Big Brother, The Matrix, San Francisco.

October 6, 1967: Big Brother, with Jack & the Ripper, The Ark, Sausalito, California.

October 7 & 8, 1967: Big Brother, Avalon Ballroom, San Francisco.

October 8, 1967: Big Brother, Haight-Ashbury Medical Clinic Benefit, Family Park, San Jose.

October 13 & 14, 1967: Big Brother, with Moby Grape, The Ark, Sausalito, California.

October 15 & 16, 1967: Big Brother, Avalon Ballroom, San Francisco.

October 28 & 29, 1967: Big Brother, Peacock Country Club, San Rafael, California.

November 1967: Big Brother signs with manager Albert Grossman.

November 2–4, 1967: Big Brother, with Pink Floyd and Richie Havens, Fillmore / Winterland, San Francisco.

November 4, 1967: Big Brother, with Moby Grape, The Ark, Sausalito, California.

November 13, 1967: Big Brother, with the Grateful Dead and Quicksilver Messenger Service, Avalon Ballroom, San Francisco.

November 23 & 24, 1967: Big Brother, with Friendly Stranger, California Hall, San Francisco.

November 25, 1967: Big Brother, with Mount Rushmore, Avalon Ballroom, San Francisco.

December 1967: Big Brother plays gigs in Fresno, Turlock, Merced, and other towns in California's San Joaquin Valley, as well as the Golden Bear in Huntington Beach.

December 15 & 16, 1967: Big Brother, Whisky A Go Go, Los Angeles.

December 28, 1967: Big Brother Christmas party, Sokol Hall, San Francisco.

December 29 & 30, 1967: Big Brother, with Chuck Berry and Quicksilver Messenger Service, Fillmore Auditorium, San Francisco.

December 31, 1967: Big Brother, with Jefferson Airplane and Quicksilver Messenger Service, Winterland, San Francisco.

[1968]

January to mid-February 1968: Big Brother, appearances in San Francisco and around California.

January 6, 1968: Big Brother, Sacramento State College, Sacramento.

January 25–27, 1968: Big Brother, with the Electric Flag and the Youngbloods, Fillmore/Winterland, San Francisco.

February 2, 1968: Big Brother, Cheetah, Los Angeles.

February 9, 1968: Big Brother, Exhibit Hall, San Diego.

February 16, 1968: Big Brother, Palestra, Philadelphia.

February 17, 1968: Big Brother, Anderson Theater, New York City — their first New York show.

February 23 & 24, 1968: Big Brother, Psychedelic Supermarket, Boston.

February 25, 1968: Big Brother, Rhode Island School of Design, Providence.

March 1 & 2, 1968: Big Brother, with MC5 and Tiffany Shade, Grande Ballroom, Detroit.

March 8, 1968: Big Brother, with Tim Buckley and Albert King, Fillmore East, New York City.

March 9, 1968: Big Brother, Wesleyan University, Middletown, Connecticut.

March 15–17, 1968: Big Brother, Electric Factory, Philadelphia.

March 22–24, 1968: Big Brother, Cheetah, Chicago.

April 2–7, 1968: Big Brother, Generation, New York City.

April 7, 1968: Big Brother, with Jimi Hendrix, Buddy Guy, Joni Mitchell, Richie Havens, Paul Butterfield, and Elvin Bishop, Wake for Martin Luther King, Jr., Generation, New York City.

April 10, 1968: Big Brother, Anaheim Convention Center, Anaheim.

April 11–13, 1968: Big Brother, with Iron Butterfly and Booker T. & the M.G.'s, Fillmore/Winterland, San Francisco.

April 11, 1968: Big Brother, appearance on ABC-TV's "Hollywood Palace."

April 13, 1968: Big Brother, Winterland, San Francisco.

April 19, 1968: Big Brother, with the Mint Tattoo, Selland Arena, Fresno, California.

April 20, 1968: Big Brother, Santa Barbara.

April 26, 1968: Big Brother, Foothill College, Los Altos Hills, California.

April 27, 1968: Big Brother, San Bernardino.

April 29 to May 9, 1968: Big Brother begins recording Cheap Thrills album in Los Angeles.

May 1, 1968: Big Brother, Chico State College, Chico, California.

May 3–4, 1968: Big Brother, with Albert King, Shrine Auditorium, Los Angeles.

May 10, 1968: Big Brother, Cal-Poly State University, San Luis Obispo, California.

May 11, 1968: Big Brother, with Bronze Hog, Veterans Hall, Santa Rosa, California.

May 12, 1968: Big Brother, with Taj Mahal and Sweetwater, San Fernando Valley State College, California.

May 15, 1968: Big Brother, with Rejoice and the Youngbloods, Hells Angels dance, Carousel Ballroom, San Francisco.

May 17, 1968: Big Brother, Freeborn Hall, University of California, Davis.

May 18, 1968: Big Brother, San Jose Fairgrounds, San Jose.

May 19, 1968: Big Brother, Pasadena.

May 20 to June 12, 1968: Big Brother records Cheap Thrills in Los Angeles, with some days off for R&R.

May 24–26, 1968: Big Brother, with the Clara Ward Singers and H. P. Lovecraft, Carousel Ballroom, San Francisco.

June 13–15, 1968: Big Brother, with the Foundations and Crazy World of Arthur Brown, Fillmore/Winterland, San Francisco.

June 16, 1968: Big Brother, with Steve Miller Blues Band, Sandy Bull, Dan Hicks, and Santana, Matrix Benefit, Fillmore, San Francisco.

June 22 & 23, 1968: Big Brother, Carousel Ballroom, San Francisco.

June 24, 1968: Big Brother, with the Peanut Butter Conspiracy, Debutante Cotillion, Burlingame Country Club, Burlingame, California.

June 28 & 29, 1968: Big Brother, Denver.

July 5, 1968: Big Brother, Concord, California.

July 6, 1968: Big Brother, Northern California.

July 7, 1968: Big Brother, Free concert, Golden Gate Park, San Francisco.

July 12 & 13, 1968: Big Brother, Kaleidoscope, Los Angeles.

July 16–18, 1968: Big Brother, with Richie Havens and Illinois Speed Press, Fillmore–Carousel, San Francisco.

July 20, 1968: Big Brother, Salt Lake City.

July 22, 1968: Big Brother, Westbury Music Fair, Long Island.

July 25, 1968: Big Brother, Columbia Records Convention, Puerto Rico.

July 27, 1968: Big Brother, Newport Folk Festival, Newport, Rhode Island.

August 1968: Columbia Records releases Big Brother's *Cheap Thrills* album, which goes on to top the charts.

August 2 & 3, 1968: Big Brother, with the Staple Singers and Ten Years After, Fillmore East, New York City.

August 9, 1968: Big Brother, Kiel Auditorium, St. Louis.

August 14, 1968: Big Brother, Monticello, Indiana.

August 16, 1968: Big Brother, Cheetah, Chicago.

August 18, 1968: Big Brother, Tyrone Guthrie Theater, Minneapolis.

August 23, 1968: Big Brother, Singer Bowl, Queens, New York City.

August 30 to Sept. 1, 1968: Big Brother, Palace of Fine Arts Festival, San Francisco; Janis announces that she will leave Big Brother at the end of fall 1968.

September 6, 1968: Big Brother, with Iron Butterfly and the Fraternity of Man, Hollywood Bowl.

September 12–14, 1968: Big Brother, with Santana and Chicago Transit Authority, Fillmore West, San Francisco.

September 15, 1968: Big Brother, with Joan Baez, the Everly Brothers, The Byrds, Country Joe and the Fish, Junior Wells, Buddy Guy, the Mothers of Invention, Buffy St. Marie, and Wilson Pickett, Rose Bowl, Pasadena.

September 27, 1968: Big Brother, University of California, Irvine.

September 28, 1968: Big Brother, San Diego.

September 29, 1968: Big Brother, taping of "Hollywood Palace" television show, Los Angeles.

October 4, 1968: Big Brother, Cleveland.

October 5, 1968: Big Brother, State University of New York, Buffalo.

October 11, 1968: Big Brother, War Memorial Auditorium, Syracuse, New York.

October 13, 1968: Big Brother, Music Hall, Cincinnati.

October 15, 1968: Big Brother, Grande Ballroom, Detroit.

October 18, 1968: Big Brother, Pennsylvania State University, State College.

October 19, 1968: Big Brother, Spectrum, Philadelphia.

October 20, 1968: Big Brother, Alexandria Roller Rink, Alexandria, Virginia.

October 25, 1968: Big Brother, Curry Hicks Cage, University of Massachusetts, Amherst.

October 26, 1968: Big Brother, Worcester Polytechnic Institute, Worcester, Massachusetts.

November 1968: Big Brother's Cheap Thrills album hits #1 in Billboard's Top 100.

November 1 & 2, 1968: Big Brother, Electric Factory, Philadelphia.

November 8, 1968: Big Brother, Warwick, Rhode Island.

November 9, 1968: Big Brother, Woolsey Hall, Yale University, New Haven, Connecticut.

November 10, 1968: Big Brother, White Plains, New York.

November 11, 1968: Big Brother, Ridge Arena, Braintree, Massachusetts.

November 12, 1968: Big Brother, Jersey City.

November 14, 1968: Big Brother, Hartford, Connecticut.

November 15, 1968: Big Brother, Hunter College, New York City.

November 16, 1968: Big Brother, State University of New York, Stony Brook.

November 23, 1968: Big Brother, Houston Music Hall, Houston.

November 24, 1968: Big Brother, Coliseum, Dallas.

November 26, 1968: Big Brother, Denver Auditorium, Denver.

November 29, 1968: Big Brother, Seattle.

November 30, 1968: Big Brother, Vancouver.

December 1, 1968: Big Brother, Family Dog Benefit, San Francisco —Janis's last gig with Big Brother.

December 21, 1968: Janis's first appearance with her new band, later to be named the Kozmic Blues Band; with the Bar-Kays, Booker T. & the M.G.'s, Albert King, Rufus and Carla Thomas, William Bell, and Eddie Floyd; Stax-Volt Records Christmas Show, Memphis.

[1969]

January 2 to February 6, 1969: Janis and the Kozmic Blues Band rehearse new material.

February 8, 1969: Kozmic Blues, New York.

February 9, 1969: Kozmic Blues, Music Hall, Boston.

February 11 & 12, 1969: Kozmic Blues, Fillmore East, New York City.

February 14, 1969: Kozmic Blues, State University of New York, Albany.

February 15, 1969: Kozmic Blues, University of Vermont, Burlington.

February 16, 1969: Kozmic Blues, Toronto.

February 21, 1969: Kozmic Blues, Colby College, Waterville, Maine.

February 22, 1969: Kozmic Blues, Clark University, Worcester, Massachusetts.

February 23, 1969: Kozmic Blues, Queens College, Flushing, New York.

February 28, 1969: Kozmic Blues, University of North Carolina, Chapel Hill.

March 1, 1969: Kozmic Blues, Duke University, Durham, North Carolina.

March 7, 1969: Kozmic Blues, Evanston, Illinois.

March 9, 1969: Kozmic Blues, Toledo, Ohio.

March 15, 1969: Kozmic Blues, blocking for "The Ed Sullivan Show" in the morning; appearance at University of Michigan, Ann Arbor, in the evening.

March 16, 1969: Kozmic Blues, appearance on "The Ed Sullivan Show."

March 20–23, 1969: Kozmic Blues, Winterland/Fillmore West, San Francisco.

March 27, 1969: Kozmic Blues, Sacramento.

March 28, 1969: Kozmic Blues, San Bernardino.

March 29, 1969: Kozmic Blues, San Diego.

March 30, 1969: Kozmic Blues, departure for Stockholm and European tour.

April 1, 1969: Kozmic Blues, taping of television show in Stockholm.

April 2, 1969: Kozmic Blues, flight to London for European tour rehearsals.

April 11, 1969: Kozmic Blues, Amsterdam.

April 12, 1969: Kozmic Blues, two concerts in Frankfurt.

April 14, 1969: Kozmic Blues, Olympia Theatre, Paris.

April 17, 1969: Kozmic Blues, Stockholm.

April 19, 1969: Kozmic Blues, Tivoli Gardens, Copenhagen.

April 21, 1969: Kozmic Blues, Albert Hall, London (sold out).

April 24, 1969: Kozmic Blues, return to the United States from European tour.

April 25, 1969: Kozmic Blues, Springfield, Massachusetts.

April 26, 1969: Kozmic Blues, MIT, Cambridge, in the afternoon; Brown University, Providence, Rhode Island, in the evening.

April 27, 1969: Kozmic Blues, Rochester, New York.

May 2, 1969: Kozmic Blues, War Memorial Auditorium, Syracuse, New York.

May 3, 1969: Kozmic Blues, Cornell University, Ithaca, New York.

May 4, 1969: Kozmic Blues, University of New Hampshire, Durham.

May 9, 1969: Kozmic Blues, Cleveland Convention Center, Ohio.

May 10, 1969: Kozmic Blues, Cobo Hall, Detroit.

May 11, 1969: Kozmic Blues, Veteran's Memorial Music Hall, Columbus, Ohio.

June 16–26, 1969: Kozmic Blues records I Got Dem Ol' Kozmic Blues Again Mama!, Los Angeles.

June 30, 1969: Kozmic Blues, St. Louis.

July 1, 1969: Kozmic Blues, Edwardsville, Illinois.

July 2, 1969: Kozmic Blues, Des Moines, Iowa.

July 5, 1969: Kozmic Blues, Atlanta International Pop Festival, Atlanta.

July 8, 1969: Kozmic Blues, Tanglewood Music Festival, Tanglewood, Massachusetts.

July 11, 1969: Kozmic Blues, Hampton Beach, New York.

July 12, 1969: Kozmic Blues, Yale Bowl, New Haven, Connecticut.

July 16, 1969: Kozmic Blues, appearance on "The Dick Cavett Show."

July 19, 1969: Kozmic Blues, Forest Hills Tennis Stadium, Queens, New York.

July 25 & 26, 1969: Kozmic Blues, Merriweather Post Pavilion, Columbia, Maryland.

August 3, 1969: Kozmic Blues, Atlantic City.

August 16, 1969: Kozmic Blues, Woodstock Music & Art Fair, Bethel, New York. Other performers on the 16th: Canned Heat, Creedence Clearwater Revival, the Grateful Dead, Keef Hartley, Jefferson Airplane, Mountain, Quill, Santana, The Who.

August 23, 1969: Kozmic Blues, Convention Hall, Asbury Park, New Jersey.

August 27, 1969: Kozmic Blues, Saratoga Performing Arts Camp, Saratoga Springs, New York.

August 29, 1969: Kozmic Blues, Blossom Music Festival, Cuyahoga Falls, Ohio.

August 30, 1969: Kozmic Blues, Texas International Pop Festival, Dallas International Speedway, Dallas.

August 31, 1969: Kozmic Blues, Louisiana International Speedway, Gonzales, Louisiana.

September 1969: Columbia releases I Got Dem Ol' Kozmic Blues Again Mama!

September 8, 1969: Kozmic Blues, taping of "Music Scene" television show, Los Angeles.

September 18, 1969: Kozmic Blues, rehearsal for "This Is Tom Jones" television show, Los Angeles.

September 20, 1969: Kozmic Blues, Hollywood Bowl.

September 21, 1969: Kozmic Blues, taping of "This Is Tom Jones."

October 3, 1969: Kozmic Blues, Tempe, Arizona.

October 4, 1969: Kozmic Blues, San Diego Sports Arena, San Diego.

October 5, 1969: Kozmic Blues, Winterland, San Francisco.

October 11, 1969: Kozmic Blues, Sacramento.

October 17, 1969: Kozmic Blues, University of Texas, Austin.

October 18, 1969: Kozmic Blues, San Antonio.

October 19, 1969: Kozmic Blues, Houston.

October 31, 1969: Kozmic Blues, Convention Hall, Philadelphia.

November 8, 1969: Kozmic Blues, University of Tennessee, Knoxville.

November 16, 1969: Kozmic Blues, Tampa, Florida.

November 21, 1969: Kozmic Blues, Dane County Exposition Center, Madison, Wisconsin.

November 23, 1969: Kozmic Blues, Auditorium Theater, Chicago.

November 28, 1969: Kozmic Blues, Pittsburgh.

December 5, 1969: Kozmic Blues, Georgia Tech, Atlanta.

December 6, 1969: Kozmic Blues, University of Virginia, Charlottesville.

December 6, 1969: Broadcast of "This Is Tom Jones" television show with Kozmic Blues performance.

December 7, 1969: Kozmic Blues, with Butterfield Blues Band and special guest Joe Cocker, Civic Center, Baltimore.

Mid-December 1969: Janis and Kozmic Blues perform "Me and Bobby McGee" for the first time in concert, Nashville.

December 19, 1969: Kozmic Blues, Madison Square Garden, New York City, 1969 — the last Kozmic Blues Band gig.

[1970]

April 4, 1970: Janis sings with Big Brother and the Holding Company at a reunion performance, San Francisco.

Mid-May, 1970: Janis's first performance with her new band, soon to be called the Full Tilt Boogie Band; Big Brother and the Holding Company also plays, with Nick Gravenites singing lead; Hells Angels dance, Pepperland, San Rafael, California.

May 29, 1970: Full Tilt, Gainesville, Florida.

May 30, 1970: Full Tilt, Jacksonville, Florida.

May 31, 1970: Full Tilt, Miami.

June 5, 1970: Full Tilt, Columbus, Ohio.

June 6, 1970: Full Tilt, Indianapolis.

June 12, 1970: Full Tilt, Louisville, Kentucky.

June 14, 1970: Full Tilt, Kansas City.

June 19 & 20, 1970: Full Tilt, College Park, Maryland.

June 26, 1970: Full Tilt, Schenectady, New York.

June 28, 1970: Full Tilt, Festival Express first concert, Toronto. Other performers on this three-concert train tour: The Band, the Grateful Dead, Delancy and Bonnie and Friends, Ian and Sylvia, New Riders of the Purple Sage, Tom Rush, Buddy Guy, Eric Andersen, Mountain, Ten Years After, Traffic, Seatrain, Charlebois, James & the Good Brothers, Cat, Mashmakan, and the Modern Rock Quartet.

July 1, 1970: Full Tilt, Festival Express second concert, Winnipeg, Manitoba.

July 4, 1970: Full Tilt, Festival Express final concert, Calgary, Alberta.

July 5, 1970: Full Tilt, Seattle.

July 6, 1970: Full Tilt, Honolulu.

July 10, 1970: Janis appears without her band at the 70th birthday party for Ken Threadgill, the Austin club owner who gave her her first singing job.

July 11, 1970: Full Tilt, Sports Arena, San Diego.

July 12, 1970: Full Tilt, with Joy of Cooking, Santa Clara Fairgrounds, San Jose.

July 17, 1970: Full Tilt, Albuquerque, New Mexico.

August 2, 1970: Full Tilt, Forest Hills Tennis Stadium, New York City (the original date, Aug. 1, was rained out).

August 3, 1970: Full Tilt, taping of "The Dick Cavett Show."

August 5, 1970: Full Tilt, Ravinia Park, Highland Park, Illinois.

August 6, 1970: Full Tilt, Peace Festival, Shea Stadium, New York City.

August 8, 1970: Full Tilt, Capitol Theater, Port Chester, New York.

August 11, 1970: Full Tilt, Garden State Arts Center, New Jersey.

August 12, 1970: Full Tilt, Harvard Stadium, Cambridge, Massachusetts — their last concert.

August 15, 1970: Janis attends her ten-year high school reunion, Port Arthur, Texas, 1970.

September 1970: Full Tilt records the Pearl album, Los Angeles.

October 4, 1970: Janis dies of an accidental overdose of heroin in Los Angeles. The Pearl album is completed after her death by producer Paul Rothchild and the Full Tilt Boogie Band. After its release in January 1971, it goes to #1 for nine weeks and contains a hit single, Janis's version of Kris Kristofferson's "Me and Bobby McGee."

Discography

Big Brother and the Holding Company
Featuring Janis Joplin

Singles

MAINSTREAM

657	Blindman / All Is Loneliness	November 1966
662	Down on Me / Call on Me	May 1967
666	Bye, Bye Baby / Intruder	August 1967
675	Women Is Losers / Light Is Faster Than Sound	November 1967
678	Coo Coo / The Last Time	February 1968
662	Down on Me / Call on Me *(reissue, using the same catalog number)*	July 1968

COLUMBIA

44626	Piece of My Heart / Turtle Blues	August 1968
45284	Keep On / Joseph's Coat	December 1970
45284	Keep On / Home on the Strange	January 1971

Albums

MAINSTREAM

6099	Big Brother and the Holding Company	August 1967

COLUMBIA

9700	Cheap Thrills	August 1968
30222	Be a Brother *(with Janis doing backup vocals)*	November 1970
30631/P-13313	Big Brother and the Holding Company *(Columbia Special Products reissue of Mainstream 6099)*	April 1971

MADE TO LAST

001	Cheaper Thrills	1984

Solo Recordings Singles

COLUMBIA

45023	Kozmic Blues / Little Girl Blue	November 1969
45080	Try (Just a Little Bit Harder) / One Good Man	February 1970
45128	Maybe / Work Me, Lord	April 1970
33183	Piece of My Heart / Kozmic Blues *(Columbia Hall of Fame reissue series)*	November 1970
45314	Me and Bobby McGee / Half Moon	January 1971
33208	Cry Baby / Mercedes Benz *(Columbia Hall of Fame reissue series)*	April 1971
45379	Cry Baby / Mercedes Benz	May 1971
45433	Get It While You Can / Move Over	August 1971
33205	Me and Bobby McGee / Get It While You Can	March 1972
45630	Down on Me *(live)* / Bye, Bye Baby *(live)*	July 1972

Albums

COLUMBIA

9913	I Got Dem 'Ol Kozmic Blues Again, Mama	September 1969
30322	Pearl	January 1971
30322	Pearl *(with a "CQ" prefix, quad issue)*	November 1971
31160	Joplin in Concert *(live with Big Brother and Full Tilt)*	May 1972
32168	Janis Joplin's Greatest Hits	July 1973
33345	Janis *(original soundtrack recording)*	May 1975
37569	Farewell Song	February 1982
48845	Janis *(boxed CD set)*	November 1993

I was a sophomore at U.C. Berkeley in 1967, and I fell asleep every night listening to KMPX. One night, I was half asleep when the disc jockey said that Janis had lost her dog, would anyone who knew where it was call her at . . . and he gave out her home phone number! I wrote it down despite the fact that I did not know the whereabouts of her dog.

The Avalon Ballroom postcard announcing the next concert showed up. Canned Heat and Big Brother, June 8, 9, 10, and 11. I began to contemplate calling Janis Joplin to ask her to dance. But I was wavering. Then on a Sunday afternoon, "Call on Me" came over the airwaves:

I dialed Janis's number. The first sound I heard was a line from the song — Janis was listening to herself on KMPX!

"Hello?"

I didn't know what to say, so I mumbled something like, "Hi, Janis" — pause — "you don't know me, but I'm a big fan of yours, and — uh — I was wondering if you'd dance with me at your next gig at the Avalon."

She was very down-to-earth and very direct. "Hey, man, why don't you just ask me at the dance?"

"Yeah, I could do that." I felt sort of stupid.

The night of the concert came. Big Brother played first (with a short introductory routine by the Congress of Wonders). I could hardly wait for Canned Heat's set. I positioned myself near the stage so I could ask Janis to dance as soon as she got off.

Then the set was over. I found Janis as she left the stage, introduced myself and asked her to dance. But she couldn't. Big Brother had just finished a soundtrack for an underground film and they were going to the cast party. She'd be back just before Big Brother's last set.

Just as Canned Heat started its last song, Janis reappeared. This time I asked, and she said sure. We danced a free-form boogie, then her manager came up, tapped her on the shoulder.

"Thanks for the dance," she said. "I've got to go on."

What a night!

— Peter Liepman

Notes

MISFRYIN'
PATHWAY
JOE'S SONG
FLOWER & THE SUN
30 POUND MOSES
I ___ my?

Wednesday
11ᵒᵈ Am.

*
*
*

HESITATION BLU
* ONE DAY TICKET
INTRUDER (2)
WOMEN IS LOSE

Stay tuned

park by himself — he got hit by a car. But the vet said he wasn't hurt ~~too~~ very badly — bruised & scared. Poor thing, he's just moping around with a very paranoid look on his face.

I'm having a few clothes made for me now — had a beautiful dress made out of a madras bed-spread & now she's working on one out of green crepe with a very low V-neckline. I've been making things out of leather ~~lately~~ lately. Made a beautiful blue & green garbo hat & a pair of green shoes.

blue

green

& blue beads

blue

& green beads

They're old — their style — buttons up the

when I get ba to rent a se & make mys of beautiful dress to go w

HOWDJA LIKE A FAVOR DE that has yo to send me thought of a things I'd — if they're st I'll list the